Train You

Association of Pet Dog Trainers, UK (APDT, UK)

For UK order enquiries: please contact Bookpoint Ltd,
130 Milton Park, Abingdon, Oxon OX14 4SB.
Telephone: +44 (0) 1235 827720. Fax: +44 (0) 1235 400454.
Lines are open 09.00–17.00, Monday to Saturday, with a
24-hour message answering service. Details about our titles and
how to order are available at www.teachyourself.com

For USA order enquiries: please contact McGraw-Hill Customer
Services, PO Box 545, Blacklick, OH 43004-0545, USA.
Telephone: 1-800-722-4726. Fax: 1-614-755-5645.

For Canada order enquiries: please contact McGraw-Hill
Ryerson Ltd, 300 Water St, Whitby, Ontario L1N 9B6, Canada.
Telephone: 905 430 5000. Fax: 905 430 5020.

Long renowned as the authoritative source for self-guided learning –
with more than 50 million copies sold worldwide – the **Teach Yourself**
series includes over 500 titles in the fields of languages, crafts, hobbies,
business, computing and education.

British Library Cataloguing in Publication Data: a catalogue record
for this title is available from the British Library.

Library of Congress Catalog Card Number: on file.

First published in UK 2005 by Hodder Education, part of
Hachette UK, 338 Euston Road, London NW1 3BH.

First published in US 2005 by The McGraw-Hill Companies, Inc.

This edition published 2010.

Previously published as *Teach Yourself Dog Training*.

The **Teach Yourself** name is a registered trade mark of
Hodder Headline.

Typeset by MPS Limited, A Macmillan Company.

Printed in Great Britain for Hodder Education, an Hachette UK
Company, 338 Euston Road, London NW1 3BH, by CPI Cox &
Wyman, Reading, Berkshire RG1 8EX.

The publisher has used its best endeavours to ensure that the URLs
for external websites referred to in this book are correct and active
at the time of going to press. However, the publisher and the
authors have no responsibility for the websites and can make no
guarantee that a site will remain live or that the content will remain
relevant, decent or appropriate.

Hachette UK's policy is to use papers that are natural, renewable
and recyclable products and made from wood grown in sustainable
forests. The logging and manufacturing processes are expected to
conform to the environmental regulations of the country of origin.

Impression number   10 9 8 7 6 5 4 3 2 1

Year   2014 2013 2012 2011 2010

This book is dedicated to the memory of John Fisher – a very special man who took the time to understand dogs.

Acknowledgements

With grateful thanks to Barry Eaton, Carrie Evans, C. C. Guard, Geraldine Thomas, Julia Harbord, Paddy Driscoll, Patsy Parry, Pauline Wise, Sandra Fraser, Sarah Whitehead, Stella Bagshaw and Val Harvey who wrote the original APDT *Teach Yourself Dog Training* book. It has been revised by Chris Mancini and Val Harvey.

The APDT would like to pay special thanks to Anita Stafford-Allen for providing the artwork for this book.

Image credits

Contents

Only got a minute?

Modern dog training has moved on in leaps and bounds in recent years, and we are now able to teach our dogs a tremendous variety of tasks using kind, effective techniques. This gives a dog the opportunity to work out for itself what is required, with no compulsion of any kind being necessary.

Once dogs understand the concept of these modern training methods – and believe me, they grasp it extremely quickly – we are able to teach them a huge variety of tasks. As well as the usual tricks like 'give a paw' and 'roll over', they can open and shut doors, retrieve items, search for drugs, search for people; they are used in the early detection of some kinds of cancer, and they can even be taught to read! Basically you can now teach a dog pretty much anything you want to as long as it is within your dog's physical and mental capabilities. Most of the forward-thinking dog charities including 'Hearing

Dogs' and 'Dogs for the Disabled' use these modern methods. This means they are able to effectively train the dog with the required skills, and can then easily transfer them to the control of the disabled owner.

Owners must always remember, though, that dogs are dogs and must ensure they get plenty of outlets for being doglike. This includes going for walks, sniffing interesting scents, meeting other dogs and engaging in play with their owner. The plus side is that once they have finished playing with their toys you can ask them to pick them up and put them away! Most importantly, training in this way means you can build up a fantastic bond with your dog, and all the family, including children, can have fun training their pet.

5 Only got five minutes?

Thanks to modern developments in dog training techniques, you as an owner are now able to teach your dog (or dogs) a tremendous variety of pleasurable, and often useful tasks, by kind and effective means. Such training aims to give the dog the opportunity to work out for itself what is required – with no compulsion of any kind. This not only means that once the dog has worked out how to elicit a reward from you, he is keen to try again; it also means that the behaviour will become firmly established in his mind. Even if you did not ask your dog to repeat that behaviour for many months he will – with very little prompting – remember exactly what it was you wanted him to do! Dogs learn by consequences, that basically everything they do in life has a consequence, good and bad for the dog, and how your dog perceives these 'experiences' will influence his learning – whether he will repeat a behaviour or not.

To effectively teach our dogs to do things, we need to understand how a dog learns. This means remembering he is a dog first and foremost. He sees things differently from us. He does things like greeting other dogs by sniffing their bottoms, rolling in fox poo, digging in the garden, taking things. Some dogs enjoy barking a lot. These are all things that dogs find rewarding and will repeat again and again despite us telling them not to! So whenever your dog or puppy does something you don't want him to do, think about why he is doing it, and what he might be getting out of it. If he has stolen the remote control and run off with it, a common reaction from us is to get up and chase the dog to try and retrieve it. 'Hey', your dog will think. 'That was a result, there was I, bored, while my owner sits watching the telly and wow, just picked up that thing with buttons on and it resulted in a great game of chase!' So you have just been taught by your dog to chase him – and there are few things a dog loves more than a great game of chase.

So that brief example shows you how easy it is for your dog to learn to do things you don't want him to do. The good news is that it is even easier to teach him to do things you *do* want him to learn. The easiest, quickest and most fun way to teach your dog is through 'clicker training'. It is a small box that makes a click, and once introduced to the dog he learns that the clicker has meaning because some kind of reward is about to follow. We then use this to mark behaviours we want to teach him. We are able to teach him a huge variety of tasks, as well as the usual tricks like 'paw' and 'roll over'. He can learn useful things like opening and shutting doors, retrieving items, searching for drugs, searching for people. Dogs are used in the early detection of some kinds of cancer, and they can even be taught to read! These days, the ability to train your dog can now extend to almost anything you want to teach him, as long as it is within your dog's physical and mental capabilities.

But the most important thing you'll find, by training this way, is the fantastic bond you will create with your dog; and all the family, including children, can have fun joining in.

10 Only got ten minutes?

If you want to train your dog not only to perform various tasks and tricks, walk nicely on a lead and come back to you when called; but also to live with you as part of the family and be a pet that you are happy to take with you wherever you may want to go, then training him by using positive, kind and effective methods is the easiest way to achieve your aim. Dogs learn by consequences, meaning that everything they do in life has a consequence for them, good or bad. How your dog perceives these 'experiences' will influence his learning – whether he will repeat a behaviour or not.

To effectively teach our dog to do things, we need to understand how a dog learns. This means remembering that he is a dog first and foremost. He sees things differently from us. He does things like greeting other dogs by sniffing their bottoms, and rolling in fox poo; digging in the garden and stealing things; some dogs enjoy barking a lot. These are all things that for their own reasons, dogs find rewarding and will repeat again and again, despite us telling them not to! So whenever your dog or puppy does something you don't want him to do, think about why he is doing it and what he might be getting out of it. If he has stolen the remote control and run off with it, a common reaction from us is to get up and chase the dog to try and retrieve it. 'Hey', your dog will think. 'That was a result, there was I, bored, while my owner sits watching the telly and wow, I just picked up that thing with buttons on and it resulted in a great game of chase'. So you have just been taught by your dog to chase him – and there are few things a dog loves more than a great game of chase.

So that brief example shows you how easy it is for your dog to learn to do things we don't want him to do. It is even easier to teach him to do things you *want* him to learn. First, we need to remember that there are four 'golden rules' when training a dog:

- The first one is consistency – this means that everyone involved in training your dog has to be fair to him and consistent with the rules or boundaries you decide as a family to set out for him. It may be that you don't want him to go upstairs. It is only fair that everyone complies with this rule so you dog is able to understand what is expected of him.
- The second rule is reward behaviour you want repeated – sit before food means the food is delivered, sit before lead on means you go for a walk, don't jump up, and you will say hello to him, and so on.
- Any behaviour you don't want rewarded, *ignore* – if the dog jumps up, turn away and blank out the dog; and as soon as he has four paws on the floor, you can talk to him. If he is barking for some food, turn your back and walk away; come back when he is quiet and then he can have his food. Dogs hate to be ignored and this is an extremely effective way of teaching your dog not to perform behaviours you don't want.
- If you can't ignore your dog because he is doing something that may be dangerous – chewing through an electric cable for example – then distract the dog, call him away and ask him to do something you can reward, and remove the cable from his reach.

The most important thing to remember when training a dog is that they don't deliberately do things wrong. They are not trying to get one over us or be 'pack leader' – they are simply being dogs and are unaware of what we humans find acceptable or not. We need to control the environment they live in until they understand what we want. Dogs are opportunists and if you leave the roasting joint on the worktop, and your dog has the opportunity to eat it he will do so, and find it so enjoyable that he will learn to look out for these 'treats' being left lying around more often.

The easiest, quickest and most fun way to teach your dog is through 'clicker training'. This is a small box that makes a click, and once introduced to the dog he learns that the clicker has meaning because some kind of reward is about to follow. We then use this to mark behaviours we want to teach him. (If you

can spare longer than ten minutes, there's more about clickers in
Chapter 8.)

Nowadays we are able to teach dogs a huge variety of tasks. As
well as the usual tricks like 'paw' and 'roll over' they can learn
really useful things like opening and shutting doors and retrieving
items; and perform vital services by searching for drugs and
explosives, or searching for people at disaster scenes. Some dogs
are used in the early detection of some kinds of cancer; others
can even be taught to read! Modern training techniques can now
enable you to teach a dog pretty much anything you want to as
long as it is within his physical and mental capabilities.

Above all, though, the positive relationship that you'll establish
with your dog by training him in this way will pay rich rewards in
the fun and quality time that all the family – including children –
will enjoy.

History of the Association of Pet Dog Trainers

Most people are unaware that dog training instructors are not regulated – in the way driving instructors or veterinary surgeons are – and no qualifications are required by a person who sets up as a dog training instructor. This means that there are very different levels of knowledge and understanding and very different approaches of the instructors.

In 1993 John Fisher and a group of like-minded people met to set up the Association of Pet Dog Trainers. John Fisher became the Chief Executive. One of his first tasks was to find out what pet dog owners wanted from their trainers. It had been decided that all instructors who wanted to join the Association would be assessed against stringent criteria before being given membership. Sixty people throughout the country were selected through John's personal knowledge of their activities, or other highly respected people in the dog world, to be the first assessors. These 60 elected a steering group by postal ballot of five people to lay foundations and report back. This steering group arranged draft copies of the Code of Practice, Constitution, application forms and other documentation.

The first Annual General Meeting (AGM) was held in September 1995 in Cambridgeshire, when the steering group handed over to the first elected Committee according to the constitution. C.C. Guard was elected Chairman; John Fisher and Sarah Whitehead were to be executives in charge of developing the future of the APDT. At last the APDT was able to offer pet owners and veterinary surgeons a guarantee of quality when looking for a training class or help with training a difficult dog in the area where they lived.

Sadly, John Fisher died on 18 February 1995 and it was left to C.C. Guard and Sarah Whitehead to continue nurturing John's baby into adolescence.

Members of the APDT were assessed according to the strict Code of Practice drawn up by the members themselves at the AGM, and which contains the words 'condemning such equipment as check/ choke chains, prong or spike collars, electric shock devices in any form, and high frequency sound devices which are designed to startle.'

All prospective members of the APDT still undergo a thorough assessment of their knowledge and ability to instruct owners in the training of their dogs. If the applicant meets the criteria and agrees to abide by the APDT Code of Practice, they are offered membership and the right to use the APDT logo. Members also agree to continue their education and keep up to date with modern training methods and ideas.

Summer 1995 saw the first directory printed by the APDT, which was sent to all the veterinary practices in the UK so that vets have details of members in their area. With the increased popularity of the internet the directory was replaced in 2008 by pages on the APDT website. This gives dog owners, behaviourists and vets access to members' details.

The APDT works in partnership with James Wellbeloved and their sponsorship enables us to promote 'Kind, Fair and Effective' training for dog owners in the UK.

Pet owners can be certain that no coercive or punitive techniques and equipment will be used by members, as these are contrary to the Code of Practice. Any member who is charged with contravening this code is thoroughly investigated via a stringent complaints process. If the allegation is upheld their membership is withdrawn.

If you would like to understand and train your dog, then this book should help. If you are able to attend classes, or need extra help, look for an APDT training instructor on www.apdt.co.uk

1

Principles of dog training

In this chapter you will learn:
- *what makes your dog tick*
- *how to motivate your dog*
- *how to train effectively*.

How dogs learn

AT THE BEGINNING

From the day your dog was born he was learning. From the very
first struggle to find a teat to get milk, the very first attempts at
play, the first squeal or bark, what happened as a consequence was
beginning to dictate how that pup was going to develop into an
adult dog. By the time you got your puppy at seven or eight weeks
old the learning had already started, and his early rearing and
development will have already had an impact. If you have taken on
an adult dog, then more learned behaviour is firmly established –
good and bad. Whatever the age of dog you have taken on, you
aren't starting with a blank sheet.

THE GENETIC INPUT

The genes your dog was born with make a difference to how he
responds to, or learns from, events. Dogs are usually born with
breed-specific characteristics; for example, German Shepherds are
more likely to want to guard and Retrievers are more likely to want

to carry articles around. Some may be less obvious, like Cavalier King Charles Spaniels who can have strong retrieving instincts; a remnant of their gundog ancestry. Dogs also have specific traits inherited from both the dam and the sire. It might be something as insignificant as the way a dog cocks his head or barks. But it can also be a tendency to be aggressive, energetic, obsessive or some other characteristic. These kinds of characteristics can influence how your dog learns and what you might need to teach him.

Insight

Your dog's genes can influence how he learns and what you need to teach him.

It is debatable how much we humans have altered the original wolf, but there are plenty of traits that have been enhanced either by accident or design, which suit us. Some traits have been weakened – either by natural selection or by our active intervention – and some have been enhanced.

Border Collies, for example, have been bred for many generations to want to work obsessively and be very single minded in their work. They have been bred to have ultra-high speed reactions. But these traits, while excellent for training for competitive sports requiring agility, can make life difficult in a family home and a Border Collie in a domestic situation needs a lot of investment in training and exercise. A dog that has been bred for many generations to display very strong genetic traits is going to be hard to train to stop displaying them, whether it's a Springer Spaniel wanting to put his nose down and search or a terrier wanting to kill small furry creatures.

On the other hand we have developed plenty of breeds that have their chase and hunting instincts reduced (but never removed entirely); for example, the French Bulldog, the Rough Collie or the Newfoundland. A liking for dogs as cute, possibly even precocious, companions, which don't demand huge amounts of exercise, has led us to breed many toy breeds such as the Bichon Frise, and the Toy or Miniature Poodles. They are likely to be less single minded than the average Border Collie, but are likely to be more 'creative' and independent.

Some breeds have more specific behaviours, which may have happened almost by accident. Many of the Spitz breeds (but not all) have a strong tendency towards barking, for example. You will find it a lot harder to teach your average Finnish or German Spitz to be quiet than your average English Setter.

However, it's not all bad news. It's these very traits that can make training easier for us if we use them to our advantage. The basic instincts for hunting and chasing, as well as the desire to be part of a social group, all make our job easier.

What these traits mean is that you can have an expectation of how your dog *might* behave. It helps you predict what his training needs *might* be, in addition to those you have identified already. But don't let your preconceptions about what you are told about your dog's breed, or genes, limit you and what you want to teach your dog. One of the greatest disservices owners do to their dogs is in assuming their breed is different from all other dogs and they therefore cannot learn certain things.

Of course, if you have a rescue dog of unknown parentage you have no helpful pointers except guesswork. It adds to the fun of training; trying to work out where your dog's traits might have come from and what breeds can be detected. But at the end of the day it doesn't matter. Your dog is a unique and independent animal who is his own 'person' and that is the dog you are training. You aren't training a collection of genes.

VIVE LA DIFFÉRENCE

You probably realize that no two dogs are the same. Also what you want from your dog may be different from another family. It is for you to decide what you want when training your dog, and although this book covers the basics you may not want to teach your dog all of them. That's fine! The collective experience of APDT members is that these are the exercises that are most asked for and needed by dog owners. But training isn't just about following a recipe or following instructions. It's about understanding *your* dog and matching his and your needs.

For example, if your dog is very lively and energetic and you would like him to be calmer, you might want to teach him to relax and settle down before you teach him to fetch a ball. Whereas if you have a more laid-back puppy you might want to put more emphasis on teaching him to want to run about and play games before you worry about teaching him a sit stay.

THE HUMAN/CANINE INTERFACE

The basic blueprint of the wolf is often used as a model of how we should train our dogs. Dogs do share basic behaviours with wolves and other *canids*, and we ignore them at our peril – most pet dogs have some tendency to want to chase, growl, dig and compete for food, for example, whatever the breed. But the importance of understanding a wild wolf pack structure when *teaching* our family pet dogs how to behave in our human world is largely overstated.

Insight
Dogs are dogs, and people are people – we need to learn to understand each other.

Dogs come to us with dog behaviour – this is genetically very similar to wolves – but neither wolf nor dog behaviour helps our dogs understand human language or behaviour. Every dog has to learn every human signal or cue (command). We humans can only be human (not dogs and not wolves). Our values, language and development are different. Dogs cannot emulate people. Dogs can never learn a human moral outlook. It is doubtful that they ever learn our language other than as cues to actions or consequences. They can only learn the meaning of a word such as 'sit', for example, if we then teach them that if they put their bottom on the floor, that action has a consequence (a reward). And if they don't put their bottom on the floor when asked, that has a consequence too (no reward).

Even when your dog understands cues or commands, he then has to want to do as asked.

Dogs, like us, will work to gain things they want, or work to avoid things they don't like. The APDT ethos is to train with the former, and work hard to avoid the latter. Dogs learn to do things (or stop doing things) through what is advantageous to them and what is disadvantageous. They can never learn it is wrong, in a moral sense, to bite people or chase livestock, or that it is right to come when called or not jump up. They can, however, learn that they get something good (food, game, praise, fuss) when they do something we ask of them.

CONTROL THE ENVIRONMENT

The job we have in training our dogs is to help them understand what we want of them, taking the trouble to understand what they are saying to us. It shouldn't be a one way 'me master – you slave' relationship, but one of you has to be in control of events and if it's the dog, then you are in trouble! The knack in training is for you, the owner, to control the environment in which your dog lives. To supply consequences to actions, and manage things so your dog cannot get things terribly wrong. And finally, to teach him the meanings of certain words and signals.

Training will never teach your dog to stop wanting to behave like a dog. Dogs are independent, thinking creatures with motivations and emotions that all too often conflict with what we want of them. You must be realistic about your expectations. Dogs have natural drives, which demand they find food and find a mate. All training does is shift the odds in your favour so that you can stop your dog following those drives when you don't want him to. Castrating a male dog will dramatically improve those odds if he is fighting other male dogs or escaping in order to look for bitches. But don't let those expectations limit you and what you can try and achieve. You may not get a 100 per cent reliable recall from a lurcher, but if you don't try, you definitely won't succeed.

Some old-fashioned training techniques rely on punishing dogs for unwanted, but natural, dog behaviours, but it is better to manage things so your dog cannot do them, or teach him an alternative behaviour which can be rewarded. One luxury we pet dog owners have is that we *can* control our dog's environment and we can, by using leads, fences and doors, limit our dogs' choices so they are not put at risk.

Motivation

REWARDS

Many dog trainers and owners talk about 'rewards'. Technically speaking, when we talk about rewards we should be talking about 'reinforcement'. The psychology textbooks describe reinforcement as anything that 'increases, or strengthens, a behaviour'. Broadly speaking, reinforcement is what causes your dog to *choose* to repeat something like coming when called, or sitting when asked. But it's not just about us consciously supplying a reward as some kind of payment for a correctly carried out action. Much of it is accidental. A dog is very quick to spot a situation which is to his benefit and it's one of the reasons why dogs have been so successful as a species in our human environment. For instance, a dog may sit close to you in the kitchen when you prepare food if he learns that some scraps might fall on the floor. That 'sitting next to Mum' action is being *reinforced* by food falling on the floor.

A reinforcer, or reward, is usually something nice, like a food treat or a game, or fuss from an owner. On the whole, although there are exceptions, pet dogs and especially pups want attention, food and play. It's your *dog's* definition of reward that is important here, not yours, so you will need to know what turns your dog on.

Special food treats are usually top of the list. Games may be more difficult as some dogs have to be taught how to enjoy playing, much as we need to if we are to enjoy a game, whether it's soccer, Monopoly or tug-of-war. But once learned, and used effectively, play can be a powerful reinforcer. Attention is usually desirable to a dog because it is often paired with something else. We tend to give them attention when we play a game with them, or give them their dinner or a food treat. Some dogs like affection and a fuss, but it often isn't high on the list of desirable rewards for many dogs. It's often we owners who like giving a dog a stroke and a pat more than some dogs like receiving them!

Reinforcement isn't just about being nice to your dog, it's about you giving one of those things, which your dog actively wants, as a consequence to your dog's action, which makes it more likely the action will be repeated in the future.

Insight
Reinforcement – giving your dog something he actually wants.

PRACTICAL APPLICATION OF REINFORCEMENT (REWARDS)

How do you use reinforcement in training your dog? Before you can give your dog a reward (and reinforce the behaviour), your puppy or dog has to do the action. You can't get your dog to do more of something if he isn't doing it in the first place!

There are different ways you can engineer your dog into doing things so they can be reinforced. Luring with a food treat works best for some exercises, like a sit or a down, for instance. But your dog will need to learn (as will you) how to use a food lure effectively. It is not unusual for an adult dog that has never been trained using food to not want to follow a food lure, so he may take a little longer to learn. It can take a few attempts, but persevere because it will make so much of the training easier.

A food lure is any small, tasty treat that your dog enjoys. It is a simple way of helping your dog into position by asking him to follow your hand until he is in the right position (see Chapters 6 and 8 for details on how to achieve this).

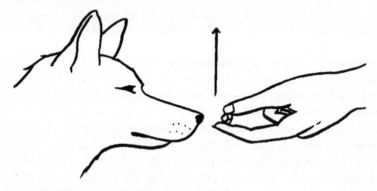

Figure 1.1 How to lure a dog with a good treat.

You can use a food lure for teaching your dog to:

▶ *sit*
▶ *lie down*
▶ *stand*
▶ *roll over*
▶ *twirl*
▶ *follow you.*

Stick to either the right or the left hand for now. Don't chop and change to start with. If you want to go on to do any kind of obedience competitions with your dog, or know you will be going into a class which progresses to that standard, it is probably best if you use the left hand, but otherwise it doesn't matter which.

Once he is confident about following the lure, start to move your dog with a bit more energy, encouraging him to show a bit more enthusiasm for this 'game'. One of the ways to stop training becoming boring is to bring a bit of movement into the picture, and how you move your dog with a food lure can help do that.

Below are some other ways of helping your dog to learn a behaviour or cue.

BODY LANGUAGE

Luring with food isn't the only way to get your dog to act in the way you want. The way you use your body language can work well, and the chances are you are already doing that. For instance, in calling your dog to you, crouching down, running away or waving your arms may encourage your dog to come to you. Your dog will pay a lot of attention to your body language – probably much more than you realize initially. Most of us are not aware of little movements we make, but your dog will be. Take the recall exercise – the dog is asked to sit and wait while the handler walks a distance away. The biggest problem with this exercise is that the dog will return to the handler before being called. To prevent this anticipation (of the recall cue) the handler will walk away, turn and wait for a few seconds to call their dog. This is to prevent the dog recognizing the handler turning as his cue to return. This is a good idea and it works well. However, what you might notice is that just before the handler calls their dog they do a small dip of the head, a movement with their hand or straighten their foot. The handler probably doesn't even realize that they are doing it; they will swear they are standing still. But the dog notices and soon interprets this small movement as his cue to return. The handler can't understand why the dog has suddenly become disobedient! Of course he hasn't – he is responding to the cue he has (albeit inadvertently) been given by the handler.

Body language can be useful in many ways when communicating with your dog. A hand movement (visual cue) to ask your dog to 'down', open arms to recall, a spin of the hand to ask for a roll over, all of these are useful cues. If your dog is at a distance from you, if he is deaf, or indeed if he goes deaf when he gets older, visual cues work better than verbal ones – but do not criticize him for responding to your body language just because you did not intend him to notice it!

SHAPING AND CAPTURING

Sometimes, 'shaping' – when you ask your dog to get closer and closer to the final desired result; or 'capturing' – when you reward your dog for something he does without being asked – are the best ways to teach your dog something. Chapter 6 looks at how to teach specific exercises and Chapter 8 looks at clicker training, which will cover some aspects of this. But the goal is always the same. Get your dog doing the action, somehow, give him a clear 'marker' as he does the action to tell him the he has done something you want, and reward. Since your dog has no knowledge of English, until taught, there is no point giving your dog a cue until he can consistently do the action. That comes later.

Effective training uses all of these methods to our advantage. However, success not only relies on knowing what your dog wants – it is also vital that your dog understands which action earned the reward.

MARKING A BEHAVIOUR

It is important that your dog understands exactly what he is being rewarded for. Perhaps you are teaching him 'sit' – he will look at you, look at the treat, follow the treat with his nose, lift his head up, put his bottom on the floor, watch the treat (and who knows how many other things like wagging his tail, blinking …). So how does he know which one of these numerous actions actually earned the reward? We 'mark' the behaviour. In the example above, we are rewarding the dog for putting his bottom on the floor; so as his bottom goes down you should say 'good' (or whatever your marker word is), and then give him his reward. Initially the word will mean nothing to your dog, but if it is always followed by a reward he will soon realize that 'good' marks the required behaviour. This will be discussed more in the section on clicker training (see Chapter 8).

PLAY REWARDS

While some dogs are naturally playful, others aren't. However, most dogs can learn to play and it's a good idea to teach them. The kind of games I am talking about are retrieving games, e.g. fetching a ball, and tugging games – pulling on a tuggie toy. It is never a good idea to encourage your puppy to play by pulling at your clothes or chasing you and the children, so steer clear of any games that encourage your dog to bite or chase people. Also, whatever games you play your dog needs to learn your rules, or he will make up his own and they may not be safe or good rules. An effective play reward is one where your dog interacts with you, with an article (e.g. a ball or tuggie toy) between you. It should be a shared activity.

WHY PLAY?

Play can be an excellent reward in training. Because it exercises your dog, less behaviour problems are likely to occur. A tired dog wants to rest, not destroy the sofa or dig holes in the garden!

If you are going to use play as a reward in training, you use it in the same way as a food treat is used. Your dog does something correctly, you tell him 'good!'; then he gets his opportunity for a game with you. You can give him a food treat as well if you like. Games are also very important for teaching your dog rules about how he should and shouldn't behave. For instance, expecting him to sit before he is given permission to go fetch a ball will teach your dog to control his instinctive desire to chase. Teaching him tuggie games (see Chapter 5) teaches him some very important rules about when to bite, what to bite and to let go of things when asked.

TEACHING 'FETCH'

Chapter 6 looks at how to teach your dog to retrieve. If you use fetching a toy as a reward during training, then it is important to keep it fun and the rules to a minimum. Throw the ball a long way, encouraging your dog to run back as fast as possible with it. If you

have a young dog or a dog with any joint problems, you may want
to check with your vet first that this amount of exercise is suitable
for your dog.

REWARD EVERY TIME THE DOG GETS
SOMETHING RIGHT

When you start to teach a particular exercise, your dog needs to
get a reward *every* time he gets it right. So if he sits when you lure
him into a sit, he gets a reward. When you fade, or vary, the lure
you also need to reward your dog every time (initially), otherwise
he will learn that no food in your hand means no reward. For every
correct action your dog needs one of his tangible, desired rewards.
A bit of sausage, the opportunity to run after a ball, or the chance
to run off-lead in the park (if allowed). It doesn't matter what the
reward is, so long as your dog actively wants it. The one reward
that we humans like to give, but is usually the least effective, is
verbal praise on its own.

Insight

Verbal praise will only be valued by your dog when the
words are associated with something your dog perceives as
a reward.

We overvalue it enormously. In reality the words mean nothing
to your dog *except* what he has learned they mean. Which isn't
'I really approve of what you have just done.' You might well
approve, but that's not the point as far as your dog is concerned!
To your dog it ought to mean 'well done! You got it right and
here's what you *really* want ... your dinner, a treat, a game ...'
Sadly, it can mean, with more traditional correction-based training,
'Well done! You just avoided a smack, a jerk on the choke chain,
or a telling off ...' Verbal praise on its own will not work long
term unless it is paired with a desired consequence for your dog.
If you do a good job at work and your boss notices and praises
you for that, it is a nice feeling. However, if, come pay day, the
boss said, 'Oh I didn't pay you for that day because I had already
told you that you had done a good job' you would feel cheated,

wouldn't you? The same applies to your dog when he is learning something.

DISPENSING WITH THE FOOD LURE

Unless you want to spend the rest of your dog's life using food (or a toy) to lure him into these positions, at some point your dog needs to understand that it isn't just following the food that is getting you to give the food to him, it's the *action* he is doing that works to get the desired consequence, i.e. that food treat. Food lure/reward training can easily go wrong if you don't get that important message across to your dog.

Once your dog has followed the food for three or four times, lure as you have been doing up to now, with your hand held in exactly the same way but with no food in your hand. When he is in position (the down, perhaps) mark his behaviour 'good', 'yes' or click, and give him his food reward that you have in your pocket, pouch or a pot. Initially the reward needs to be given very quickly after you have marked the required behaviour. You may need to be very patient the first time you try this, but remember that you have changed the cue (you have removed the food) and your dog is trying to work out what you want. If he can't work it out and does not go into the position you asked for, lure him with food one more time, then try removing the treat again. You are watching and waiting for your dog to make the decision to 'lie down' for himself. It may be hesitant, because he no longer has the prop the lure offers him, and you should be patient, but should he make the decision to lie down, reward him well.

When your dog has got to this stage you can start introducing the verbal cue if you wish.

TEACHING THE CUE

Once you can predict that your dog will reliably follow the lure (a treat or toy in your hand), and will consistently do the action you are teaching without hesitation – and hopefully with some speed and commitment – then and only then, do you introduce your word of command, or 'cue'.

Decide in advance what that cue is to be (see Chapter 4). Say it just *before* you start the luring action, count to two, then move your hand to lure your dog into position. Once he is in position, mark the action by saying 'good', 'yes' or clicking (see Chapter 8), and then give him the food treat as you have been doing over the last few sessions. Your dog is appearing to 'obey' your cue, but he has absolutely no idea what the word means, or even that it has any significance at first. If you say 'down', and he lies down when you have lured him into position, don't be fooled into thinking he has understood that 'down' means lay on the ground. He hasn't. Not yet!

Repeat that sequence of cue, pause, lure, action, reward over a few sessions, and you may find that your dog begins to realize that if he hears that sound ('down'), and he performs that action when he lies on the ground, a reward appears. When he starts to lie down before you start to lure, and it may be a very half-hearted attempt, you know he is *beginning* to understand the word! So the first time that happens, give him double rations, maybe three, and make a great fuss of him. But you may need to take a more planned approach to dispensing with the food lure.

Once your dog begins to understand your cues but is inconsistent, or doesn't obey another member of the family, it may be worth considering what your dog understands by your cue word. It isn't the word itself. A dog may not understand if the word 'sit' becomes 'sit down' in the next breath, or is said by a person with an entirely different tone of voice or accent. Sound cross and your dog may not recognize it, so the scenario in which you, the owner, gets crosser and crosser (and probably louder and louder) might mean your dog stands less and less chance of getting it right. If your dog does not understand, raising your voice and sounding 'firm' will not help. It's like shouting or speaking slower to someone who has no knowledge of English. Shouting does not aid understanding. The word 'sit' itself has no meaning for your dog, only that particular sound. Vary that sound and your dog may have no idea what you are asking of him. Don't be too quick to assume he is disobeying you. He may simply not understand.

BRIBERY?

If your dog's 'obedience' depends on you having food to hand, then your dog is only half trained. It can become a prop for both you and your dog!

At the stage where your dog is just beginning to understand a cue word, it is essential that he continues to get the reward for doing the action every time even when you don't have food in your hand, or he will learn that if you don't have food in your hand he is never rewarded. This is when a lot of dogs start to only 'obey' you when you have food, and not when you don't. From the dog's point of view it makes perfect sense. No food in hand = no reward. So why bother? It is important that the presence (or absence) of food in your hand becomes irrelevant. That rewards may appear when he carries out the action. It is not dependent on whether or not they are in your hand. It is far too easy for your dog to see the food as part of the cue and when he stops doing as asked – when you don't have food in your hand – he isn't being crafty or disobedient or stubborn, he is simply not understanding that you have changed the rules and the cue.

FADING THE REWARD

After a few training sessions on a particular exercise you are likely to be able to say your cue word, and your dog should be responding, without a luring action, although you are still rewarding every time. You are progressing well! But no one wants to have to carry food around, or throw a ball every time the dog does as he is asked. From a training point of view it's actually not very effective since experiments have shown that for an animal (whether human or dog) to respond well in the long term it is important to vary how and when the rewards appear. A lottery is a very good example of how it works. How many people who come up with the action of going to the shop and buying a lottery ticket get a reward every time? Not many! But week in, week out, they do as the advertisements suggest. Go buy a lottery ticket. It's because they *know* that the action *might* at some point have the consequence of a huge amount of money coming their way. The smaller lottery prizes, earned randomly and not in themselves very valuable, keep that belief alive. The principle of randomly rewarding the action is an essential part of the training.

Now that your dog understands which action results in the reward after a certain cue ('sit', 'down', 'buy a lottery ticket', whatever), you need to change *how* you reward. You don't reduce the rewards; just change how your dog receives them. So this time ask your dog to carry out the action, praise him (do NOT use your marking word – remember 'good', 'yes' or click is always followed by a reward at this stage), and release him from that action without giving him a treat. The chances are he will look at you expectantly, wondering where the treat is. Pretend you haven't noticed, and then ask him to carry out the action again. He should do it. His belief that you are going to reward him may be a little dented, but he should still be willing to come up with the appropriate action. Next time ask for two successful responses before you reward him. It is a mistake at this stage to make it more and more difficult to earn the treats. It's more important to keep him guessing which attempt will earn him the 'prize'. Sometimes it's the first attempt, sometimes the third. Over a few training sessions you gradually extend the number of successful repetitions of the action the dog is willing to do before you part with the rewards. Over time, you may only reward, on average, every fifth or seventh successful response to the 'sit' cue. This is an *average* – it does not mean you reward the seventh and fifth time he sits (if you do this your dog will start counting and perhaps only put an effort in for these sits). Vary the responses required – sometimes third, eighth, fourth, ninth, second and so on – so on average he is being rewarding one in five times.

OUTDOORS ... THE 'REAL WORLD!'

In all training there is an element of just making sure you build up good habits and routines. That your dog learns what 'sit' is and what he should do when the lead is being put on. That 'standing still' is what he should do when you produce a towel to dry him. Where there is no conflicting motivation often the rewards can be minimal, or virtually zero, and you may not even be aware there is 'learning' going on. If the alternative to sitting still and getting dinner as a consequence, is doing nothing and not getting his dinner, then it's an easy decision for the dog to make. Dinner or nothing? Hardly a difficult choice, is it?

However, one of the biggest problems you will have is getting your dog to respond out in the 'real world'. The 'real world' is wherever you take your dog where he is going to meet other dogs, noise, traffic, children playing football, cats, bikes, open spaces, and many other distractions. The temptations are huge and the alternatives to doing as asked are usually vastly more attractive to your dog. At home, it is very easy for your dog to learn a lot of the things you want to teach him. But outside is a different kettle of fish!

Dogs are very conscious of contexts. If he never gets rewarded in certain places for doing certain actions, then he will stop doing them in that place. Also, remember his 'obedience' isn't a moral decision on his part to comply because he thinks you are a more important 'dog' than him (wolves don't go round issuing commands to other wolves), it's a result of you conditioning him to respond to specific cues which become predictors of certain consequences. If you reward a 'sit' at home with a food treat, and never reward him at all when you are out then he will only comply with your cue at home and not when you are out, which is when so many owners start to believe the dog needs to be told off, or forced into complying. In reality you just need to take the time and trouble to reinforce what you want everywhere, not just in the front room, your garden or the dog training class.

GENERALIZATION

Dogs are very observant, but also very specific. You might think that they are only looking at the lure when they are learning to lie down, for example. So you teach your dog to 'down' in the kitchen. You no longer have food in your hand (you have 'faded the lure'); you get him responding to your hand movement or the verbal cue. Later you decide to show the family how well he has done and you go into the living room to show them. You ask the dog to 'down' and he doesn't respond. This is not your dog being disobedient. You have changed the environment – you have moved him into a different room and your dog is confused about what you want from him. This sounds a bit strange to most people – why should it make such a difference? Because he is a dog. So, what do you do? Teach your dog a behaviour in one place. Next time take him to another part of the house, and teach him again from the start; when he understands it there, move to another room and start again. Each time you move locations you will probably find that your dog understands quicker and quicker. Then it is time to take him to the garden, on a walk, in the fields, in the woods, in fact everywhere you go. In the same way if you always prepare for training by getting your treat bag, chopping up some food, putting your whistle round your neck, perhaps even putting on your 'training' clothes, your dog will soon understand 'oh, we are training'. But what happens when you are out for a walk, you have plenty of rewards in your pocket 'just in case' but no pouch, no whistle and you ask your dog to do something that he has just learned at home. He will probably look a bit confused. This doesn't mean you should not use a pouch, a whistle or comfortable shoes – all these things are very useful – but it is important that your dog understands that he does not need to see all these cues before he needs to concentrate. Just because he can't see food/toy doesn't mean that he is not going to be rewarded.

So when you are at home sometimes use your training gear, but even more often do little training sessions with your dog without the paraphernalia. Sit on the sofa and ask your dog to sit. Can he do it? If he can, reward him – the treat might be in your pocket, or in a pot on the table – if he can't, then teach him the behaviour while you are sitting down. Lay on the floor, ask him to sit – does he understand? If not, teach him, and reward him when he understands.

Until your dog responds reliably to the word 'sit' in at least ten different places, at different times of the day, with you in different positions (standing, sitting, lying down, standing on one foot), with you wearing a hat, whatever different things you can think of – then you cannot say that he understands the word. This applies to every cue you want your dog to understand – visual or verbal – and is essential in training your dog. The technical term is 'generalization'. You will find that each time you re-teach a behaviour it should take less and less time for him to learn.

Insight

It is essential that you generalize each cue you want your dog to understand.

Assuming your dog understands your cues at home, you then have to virtually re-teach that cue in other places. If your dog takes little notice of you when you ask him to do something outside, it is not that he has stopped understanding the cue, nor is he being naughty, stubborn or disobedient if he doesn't do as asked. It is that the alternatives have become irresistible and the distractions have increased tenfold. He just needs to learn that the cues he has learned at home still have the same meaning outside. Once a cue has been given it is important that he is not rewarded for any behaviour other than the one requested. This might be achieved by having him on a long line (see below). Once you have asked him to 'sit' or 'come', it's up to you to make sure it's not possible for him to do something else instead, and worse, have that incorrect action reinforced. Of course, it's important you have taught each behaviour really well at home first. Unless he will respond reliably at home, and with distractions, don't even consider trying to use those cues in the park, or on the street. All too often an owner expects a dog to come back in the park when they haven't even taught it at home. If your dog doesn't come in from the garden, from any room in the house, immediately and fast, every time you call, it is unfair and unreasonable to expect him to do so in the park. You must first teach your dog at home first everything you are going to ask of him outside.

When you do go outdoors, whatever exercise you are teaching him, initially keep your dog on a lead, or a long line attached to a fixed harness, and start with your food lures, or however you originally succeeded in teaching him at home, then reward him generously for doing as asked. He must believe that the rules are the same. If he comes up with an action, on a particular cue, then good things happen for him. If you can't get him to respond, because he is too excited, or distracted, take him to a quieter place, with fewer distractions and where it is easier to get a good result. Take it gradually, not expecting too much too soon. Whether you have a puppy or an older dog, the same rules apply. Make it easy at first in every new place, get success, and then reward him. You will need to have extra special food treats – high grade rewards. Or perhaps train outside just before the dog's normal feeding time so he is a bit hungrier than he would be just afterwards. Take his favourite toy and play with him. You have a lot of competition for his attention outside, so be ready for it and make sure that if there was a contest for 'who can win the dog's attention' you would win it. You can't force your dog to prefer you over a group of playful puppies or chasing squirrels, so you have to persuade him that you are really a much better bet and have everything those other puppies can offer, plus interest. This is where his genes are going to become more evident, as well as his early rearing. Some dogs are more gregarious than others. Some want to chase more than others. You will have to work harder at teaching and motivating your dog if he is one of them, and while you are training, keep him under control either on a lead or a long line.

It is important for your dog to learn that once you have asked for a certain action (e.g. 'come'), then only the requested action will result in a good consequence for him. Once you have called him, it must not be possible for him to run off and play with other dogs, or chase squirrels. That is where you need to manage things properly. Putting him on a long line so he can't go off and chase them will do the trick.

Worse, if you do that often enough, the cue you intend to mean one thing can come to mean exactly the opposite to your dog! It is not unusual to meet dogs who when they hear their owners say, 'Fido! Come!' run off after other dogs, because that is what they believe they should do. If they hear the cue 'come', then go off and play – a very strong reinforcer – 'come' becomes a cue to run off and play. The dog who does that, far from being disobedient, is actually doing exactly what the owner has taught. Remember, obedience is not to do with the dog having an understanding of what words mean, but what they 'cue' (what behaviour they think has been requested) and what the consequences are when they hear that word.

For training to work effectively in the outside world you need to work through the teaching stage at home so the dog understands the meaning of the cues in that context. When you start training outside you need to go through the teaching stage again in the new environment, and you need to be in control of events so your dog can't 'mislearn' or be too easily seduced by the alternatives. It's no use allowing your dog to get it wrong and you getting cross with him when it is totally within your power to make sure it doesn't go wrong.

Over a period of time, which could be days, weeks or months (depending on the dog and the exercise you are trying to teach), you need to gradually work on each exercise in slightly more distracting environments. Whether you are training a puppy or an adult dog, *every* outing is about training your dog. It's like learning to drive. You start off learning how to get the car to work and what actions you need to carry out in a quiet area, slowly concentrating on the task in hand. You don't expect to go out for a drive on a busy motorway or in busy town traffic until you have mastered the basics in quiet back roads.

FOUR QUESTIONS TO ASK YOURSELF

When training any exercise – indoors or out – there are four important questions to ask yourself:

- ▸ *What do you think you are teaching your dog?*
- ▸ *What do you think your dog is learning?*
- ▸ *What are you actually teaching your dog?*
- ▸ *What is your dog actually learning?*

For example, later on in Chapter 6 you will be told how to work with your dog on 'Watch me', where your dog looks at you, so you know he is paying attention to what you are teaching him. So what you think you are teaching is 'Watch me', what you think he is learning is to pay attention to you. Great. But look at the next question – it may be that what you are actually teaching your dog is to look at the treat pot that you are holding, ready to reward your dog. What he is actually learning is 'when the treat pot appears look at it.' There is a big difference between what you intended to teach him, and what he has actually learned!

OFF LEAD

At some point you will realize you don't need the lead or line on your dog when training outside and that he complies with your requests to do things without any help or prompting from you. Well done! Safety and the law rather than his level of training will dictate whether or not he is on lead. Of course you must never have your dog off lead near roads or livestock, and there is no kudos in showing off how well trained your dog is by letting that happen. The best trained dog can suddenly find something so distracting that he can't resist it – if there happens to be a friend on the other side of the road, and he runs across in front of a car, the consequences could be disastrous. If in doubt, be careful and keep him on lead.

Insight

Your dog should always be on a lead near a road and other dangerous areas.

NEGATIVE REINFORCEMENT AND PUNISHMENT

Sometimes, 'negative reinforcement' is used in training whereby something unpleasant is *removed* in order to get a dog to repeat an action. An example in terms of our own behaviour is when, in some cars, an annoying buzzer will sound to let you know that someone has not put their seat belt on. To stop the noise, you must fasten your seat belt. The choice is yours, but if you do not 'comply' the noise will continue. An example of this in dog training is to put physical pressure on the dog's rear end to get him to sit, and when he sits, your hand is removed. But there is no need to use any 'negative reinforcement' in training your dog. It only means the dog has to avoid something it doesn't like in order to get a reward (the cessation of the unpleasant thing). So, think about it for a moment – do you really want to do something unpleasant to your dog just so you can stop doing it? I hope not. As well as being unnecessary, this type of physical training can cause physical harm to your dog, and ruin the bond you are trying hard to build.

The word 'punishment' conjures up all sorts of bad images and ideas, mostly justified. However, scientifically speaking punishment is anything that reduces the likelihood that an action will happen again. Notice I say *reduces*. Punishments, like smacking, shaking or shouting never eliminate actions altogether; only removing the reinforcement (rewards) will do that. For instance, to reduce excessive puppy play biting, the very simple consequence of you stopping playing with the puppy is very effective. You are no longer 'reinforcing' (rewarding) the puppy's biting by continuing to play. If you were to smack or shake your pup for play biting it might well stop him doing it at that moment, but it can be just about the worst thing you can do from a long-term training and behavioural point of view. You are likely to get any number of other results in addition to your puppy stopping biting at that moment. Your puppy may start to fear you. He may start to avoid your hands. Worse, he may learn to bite harder because he feels he has to defend himself from being 'attacked' by you. He may just think what you are doing is part of the game and it could make him wilder, and bite harder. But most importantly, he won't learn 'bite inhibition' (see Chapter 5) which you may not be aware of until he is an adult, maybe years down the line. Punishments involving you, the owner, being nasty to your dog, or being aggressive, are *never* a good idea.

Punishment also has a nasty habit of escalating to abuse. Punishment can cause stress, anxiety, pain, insecurity and mistrust. As a general rule, punishments, especially physical corrections, have no place in modern dog training. There is almost invariably an alternative, desired behaviour you can reinforce which will remove the need to be unpleasant to your dog. If there isn't, then managing things so your dog can't go wrong is usually a preferred option. If your dog is in the position where you feel only a smack or a shake will work then it suggests you probably need to manage things better. If your dog is taking food from a kitchen worktop, rather than smacking your dog, why not just shut the door? Or keep food out of his reach? There is no shame in avoiding situations where you could find yourself damaging the relationship between you and your dog.

Remember, though, that it is not just physical corrections (smacking, shaking) or noise (shouting, crashing of plastic bottles) that are punishments. Ignoring your dog is also a punishment. Not giving your dog a reward when he thinks he should get one is a punishment. We use 'ignoring' and withholding of a reward to tell the dog he is doing something we do not want (you would ignore the dog when it jumps up – see Chapter 6) and that is a punishment. Try to not overuse this type of punishment either. When using ignoring or withholding rewards as punishments, remember to quickly reward him when he gets it right.

INADVERTENT LEARNING AND MOTIVATION

It's worth emphasizing that dogs are learning through both reinforcement and punishment all the time, whether or not you are involved, and they may not be learning what we think they are! Also they learn unwanted behaviour just as easily as wanted (often more easily it seems). Remember, your dog has no human moral rule book to go by, just a lot of dog genes, which drive a lot of what he wants to do.

INADVERTENT CONSEQUENCES

Understanding what is reinforcing your dog's actions is critical to sorting out behavioural problems he might have. Take 'jumping up' for instance. If your dog is jumping up at people, or you, then it is very likely that the person he is jumping up at is looking at, or touching, or fussing him. Since most dogs like attention, then this is highly likely to be reinforcing the jumping up behaviour, even if he is being told, 'Naughty boy! Get off!' The attention and touching is making the problem worse, not better. If something happens which your dog likes, then he will do it again. Later chapters look at dealing with problems like jumping up, but if you can understand the basic principle that dogs will repeat actions that are rewarded it does not take a great leap of logic to work out that they will stop those actions if they are no longer rewarded. Often a 'problem' comes from the actions your dog is carrying out being inadvertently reinforced (rewarded), if not by you, by someone else or something in the environment.

Similarly, inadvertent punishment may be stopping your dog doing something you want him to do. For instance, it is very common for owners to put the lead on their dog and finish a walk after they've called the dog to them. Even worse, some tell their dog off for not coming back quickly enough, or going off to play in the first place. Unsurprisingly, before long, the dog might avoid returning to the owner. From the dog's point of view, going back to the owner results in unwanted consequences – having the walk end and being shouted at. If your dog likes to run about off lead and hates being shouted at, why on earth would he return to you? He'd be stupid to, and dogs are rarely stupid!

Owners sometimes ask, 'Can I ever say no to my dog?' Yes, of course you can. Sometimes a dog has to be stopped fast and if your dog is doing something and you can't interrupt him by clapping then sometimes – before he is trained – you need to say 'no'. But puppies often hear 'no' so often they think it's their name! Work hard on training your dog so he understands what he needs to do instead. For example, if he is trying to pick up inappropriate food on the street teach him a 'leave it', he then understands what is required, and can act on that.

A final note on punishment, and telling your dog off – 'less is more'. Use it sparingly or it will lose its impact. Think of when your dog is growling or barking at another dog. This is a great example of where training can help. You can use 'leave it' initially, and if you know it is a behaviour that your dog often exhibits (and some dogs are intolerant of other dogs, especially if they have not been socialized when young) then you can teach him to look at you when a dog is around. Imagine this scene – a young dog growls or barks at another dog. He is not trained, does not understand 'leave it' or to look at his owner, so the owner tells him 'No'. This is a reasonable reaction. The owner is embarrassed and doesn't want her dog to get into trouble or upset the other dog. The young dog turns away, maybe even looks at his owner. So far so good, but then what I see all too often is the owner continuing to tell the dog off. What does the dog learn from this? Does he understand that he is being chastised for the growling? Almost certainly not. From his point of view he is being told off for paying attention to his owner. This is definitely not what you want to teach your dog.

THE FOUR Fs

Anything that your dog perceives as a threat elicits one of four reactions: Fight, Flight, Faffing around or Freeze.

Fight: the dog shows aggression (at varying levels) to try and make the threat go away, e.g. guarding his food bowl – he may growl when someone approaches.

Flight: the dog moves away from the threat – this might be at a run or might be a slow, tail between his legs 'slink' away. This option is removed from the dog if he is on lead, which is why dogs often show more aggression when on lead or tethered.

Faffing around/flirting (called this to keep the 'F' theme going): this is really displacement activity. The dog may exhibit puppy type behaviour, play bow, play barking, etc. or 'look for a mouse' – appear to search the ground for something that is not there, or when asked for one behaviour start offering a multitude of others.

Freeze: the dog stands still or drops into a down and stays absolutely still (apart from eye movement). This is in the hope that the perceived threat will move away, without noticing the dog. You may see this behaviour when a dog or person approaches. Some people interpret this behaviour as 'submissive' – but it is a fear-based reaction. If this doesn't work some dogs can shut down completely. This is sometimes perceived as a dog being relaxed about a situation – it is anything but. If this freeze behaviour doesn't work, and the perceived threat is still there, your dog may have no option but to show aggression.

ALPHA ROLL

The old-fashioned idea of 'alpha rolling' – when a dog would be forced onto its side or back and held down – is a good example of when a dog might initially freeze in terror, but if the threat is not quickly removed, aggression could quickly follow. Treating aggression with aggression will escalate the problem. From the dog's point of view it has to somehow get away from the threat, but freezing has not worked. Flight is not possible. Faffing around is hardly appropriate – the only option left to him is Fight. If the dog is kept pinned to the ground eventually he will shut down completely. This is where a major misunderstanding occurs – some people describe this as the dog finally submitting. If abject terror and total lack of options is submissive behaviour, then possibly they have a point.

Some dogs would freeze the first time it was done but go straight to aggression on subsequent attempted 'rolls'. All a dog learns from alpha rolling is to fear the owner, and it completely breaks down any bond the owner may have with his dog. The relationship is now based on fear rather than trust. With some dogs this can generalize to other people and children.

We would hope that if you are taking the trouble to learn about your dog by reading this book then you are not the sort of person to think of using fear as a training method, or even consider using such a cruel, outdated method as an 'alpha roll'.

The training methods outlined in this book are, mainly, 'hands off' (grooming and handling being the exceptions). We do not use hands (or leads, collars or similar) to put a dog into position. In years gone by, owners were taught to push on their dog's bottom to get them to sit. This is a method that uses 'negative reinforcement' – pressure is put on a dog's back (and sometimes also upward pressure on the lead) until the dog sits, the pressure being then released. This works on the principle that to avoid something unpleasant (the pressure), the dog performs the behaviour we require. There is no need to use anything as unpleasant as physical pressure on a dog when there are better, positive, methods available. But there are other problems apart from the possibility of damaging your dog, associated with this training method. If the cue for your dog to sit is your hand on his bottom, how is he going to know to sit if he is six feet away from you? You can't reach him, so can't give him his cue. If your dog has joint (stifle, hock, hip) or back/neck problems, these will be exacerbated by pushing on his bottom. The pain could cause him to 'refuse' to do the exercise or even bite you if he is in a lot of pain. Owners are not always aware of the problems and the first signs are when the dog acts out of character. If this occurs, do not insist your dog 'obeys' but have him checked by the vet.

CONCLUSION

You have your dog, genes and all. If he is an adult, he will have more years of learning behind him than a young puppy. But even an old dog can learn new tricks. Age is no barrier to learning although it may take longer to change old, unwanted behaviour. Your dog's type or breed may influence how he learns and his attitude to learning, but it should never be an excuse for not teaching him things he can learn and enjoy.

He needs to be taught every human signal and cue word carefully and positively, through training. In the words of dog trainer Joanna Hill: 'If a dog doesn't do as he is asked, then he either doesn't understand or he isn't motivated enough to want to do it.' Both are within our power to change.

10 THINGS TO REMEMBER

1 *Consistency is the most important thing when training your dog. Consistency in the rules of the house is probably number one for helping your dog to understand what is required of him.*

2 *Reward behaviour that you like.*

3 *Ignore behaviour that you don't like, if you possibly can.*

4 *If you can't ignore a behaviour, then interrupt, call him to you and ask him to do something you can reward.*

5 *It is important to find out what motivates your dog – this may be very different from what your friend's dog finds motivating, or what you think will be motivating.*

6 *Behaviours which your dog finds rewarding – sitting and being given a treat, being able to pull on his lead to get to the park – will be repeated. Behaviours which your dog does not find rewarding – being ignored when jumping up – are less likely to be repeated.*

7 *Dogs are opportunists. If they see a chance to get a reward, whether it is the Sunday roast, or digging a hole, they will do so. It is no good saying 'he knows he shouldn't do that'; unless your dog is 100 per cent trustworthy around food do not leave temptation in his way. This is not your dog being 'bad' or 'disobedient' – this is your dog being a dog.*

8 *Dogs come hard-wired with certain innate behaviours. This means they are pre-disposed to certain behaviours and learning some behaviours is easier than others, e.g. it is generally easier to get a Labrador to fetch a toy than it would be to get a Pug to do the same thing. They can both be trained to do this, but the Pug may take longer.*

9   *Always set your dog up for success. This would include restricting him to easily cleaned areas of the house until he is fully house-trained. Avoid leaving things laying around for your puppy to chew, and ensure that he has plenty of opportunity to sleep.*

10 *Take the trouble to find out what motivates your dog. What does he find rewarding? You might say 'food', but what sort of food? Does he like cheese more than sausage, doggie choc drops more than carrot, dried biscuit rather than liver cake?*

2

Equipment

In this chapter you will learn:
- *how to find the right equipment for your dog*
- *how to fit a head collar properly*
- *how to find the right kind of lead for your dog.*

Collars and identity tags

When in a public place a dog must, by law, *always* wear a collar with an identification tag attached that has the owner's name and address on it.

> **Insight**
> All dogs must, by law, wear an identification tag when in a public place.

It is a legal requirement and carries a £2,000 fine for non-compliance. It is a good idea to have your telephone number on it (someone finding a dog will generally phone the owner if this option is available to them). Regularly check the identity tag to ensure that it is still readable. Even if your dog is micro-chipped or tattooed he is still required to wear a tag. If you are going away and the dog is either accompanying you, or staying at a friend's, fit a barrel-type identification to his collar. With this type of tag you can write the temporary address on a piece of paper inside the barrel. It is of little use a finder phoning your home number, or taking him to your home, if he is temporarily living elsewhere.

Ensure that your dog's collar fits correctly; it should be securely fitted to prevent him slipping out of it. If it is fitted correctly you should be able to fit 2–3 fingers comfortably between the collar and your dog's neck. A collar that is too loose will slip over his head, whereas a collar that is too tight will cause rubbing and sores. Remember to check the fit of the collar regularly if you are in the habit of leaving the collar on the dog all the time. Young dogs in particular grow quickly and a collar that fits comfortably today may be tight by next week.

A collar can be made of leather, canvas or nylon fabric and will have either a buckle fastening or a plastic quick release clip. Check the condition of the collar regularly – damage to the fastening or fabric of the collar may mean that it can break at any time. If in doubt, replace it. Choke collars (which can be made of other materials beside the traditional choke-chain) have no place in modern dog training. They can cause damage to your dog's neck and back. They work by causing pain to your dog when he pulls on the lead. There is absolutely no justification, nor any need, for using pain to train a dog.

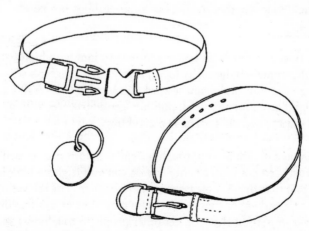

Figure 2.1 Collars and an ID tag.

TOUCHING THE COLLAR

People tend to grab dogs by their collar. This is not always a sensible thing to do as sometimes a dog may react defensively. However, it may happen, either with you or your family or a stranger. It is fair to say that your dog is going to have to have his collar felt and held to restrain him at sometime in his life, e.g. at the vet's or when you are greeting guests at the front door. There may also be a time when a stranger grabs your dog collar – he is running scared from the field, perhaps, towards a road. The stranger grabs your dog to keep him safe. Well done stranger, and thank you. But what if your dog is not used to having his collar held – or worse, if he sees it as a threat? Your dog might growl at the stranger. This person doesn't know your dog and most people, given the choice of holding on and getting bitten or letting go of a dog he has never met, will let go of your dog. I hope the situation never arises, but if it does you will be jolly glad you took the effort to help him to understand that a hand (any hand) on his collar is a good thing. For all these reasons, and for ease of putting on his lead and restraining him in various situations, it makes sense to teach him that being grabbed by the collar is a pleasant thing.

Insight
Teach your dog that having his collar grabbed is a good thing.

To do this, first touch his collar and reward him with high value rewards, something he really loves; then grab his collar a bit quicker next time and again reward him highly. Then grab his collar and give him a reward, pull him gently towards you, give him a reward and tell him he is a good boy.

When you call him to you, touch his collar before you reward him. Obviously, do not grab too quickly or you will frighten him, but teach him that this is a pleasant thing to happen. For the vet's, groomer's and anyone else's sake who may have to handle your dog, it is important that you get other people to touch his collar and not just you.

Head collars

For centuries people have understood that using a bridle on large animals, such as a cow or horse, enables us to steer and guide it rather than it pulling out of control; therefore by using a head collar we can lead from the least point of resistance.

There are various types of head collar available. Some – such as the Gentle Leader, Halti, DogAlter and Gencon – are designed to give owners more control over their dog, to stop them pulling. They work by the owner 'steering' the dog. If the dog's head is pointing left, the dog will most probably walk left, and in the same way as a rider can control a horse using a bridle, the owner can control the dog using the head collar. It is best to use a double-ended lead which has one end connected to the head collar, and the other connected to the dog's ordinary collar. The owner uses the 'collar' end in normal walking, only putting pressure on the head collar end when the dog is pulling in the wrong direction. Owners must take care not to lift the dog's head up when he is meeting another dog as this can give off a signal to the other dog that your dog is not friendly. It is imperative that a flexi-lead or long line is never used on a head collar, as the dog can run to the end of the lead and injuries can be caused if he suddenly jerks to a halt.

Insight

Never attach a flexi-lead or long line to a head collar.

Other 'head collars' are designed to cause pain to the dog – by pressing into sensitive areas of his neck (just behind his ears) when he pulls. This type of head collar has no place in modern training because any equipment that inflicts pain can lead to serious behavioural problems when used.

INTRODUCING A HEAD COLLAR TO YOUR DOG

Head collars can be useful when training your dog not to pull on his lead, or if you are a bit 'mis-matched' on size with your dog – a big strong dog who pulls on the lead, with a small owner. However, it is very unfair to simply put the head collar on the dog and expect it to be all right. Time and care *must* be taken to ensure the dog likes wearing the head collar.

- ▶ *First of all let the dog see, sniff and take food treats off the head collar.*
- ▶ *Teach the dog to put his nose through the nosepiece of the head collar for really tasty, tiny treats.*
- ▶ *When he is happy putting his nose in, gently slide the straps around his ears while he is eating the treat but do not fasten the head collar.*
- ▶ *Next time, ensuring you have some more food which he can eat with the head collar on, put the head collar on as above, fasten the clip and feed him some extra treats before taking it off.*
- ▶ *Repeat this for as many short periods as possible, gradually reducing the number of treats he eats and increasing the time the head collar is on.*
- ▶ *When your dog is happy to wear the head collar because he knows it gives him your attention and food rewards, you can extend the time further.*
- ▶ *If at any time the dog tries to scratch at the head collar, try to distract him and reward him for stopping. This means you are trying to progress too quickly.*
- ▶ *Now that your dog is happy wearing the head collar, attach a double-ended lead to it (one end on the head collar, the other on his collar) and practise walking in your home or garden.*

When he is comfortable wearing it you can use it on walks. Because you are not worried about him pulling, and the dog likes wearing the head collar, you will both find it easier to relax on your walk.

Not all dogs suit a head collar and if you have tried all the above and your dog still really dislikes it, then there are other training aids that can help you while you are teaching your dog loose lead walking.

Figure 2.2 A gentle leader and a Halti head collar.

Harnesses

There are various harnesses available; some (training harnesses) are designed to stop the dog pulling, whereas others (fixed harnesses) are simply another means of restraining the dog instead of using a collar.

TRAINING HARNESSES

These work by restricting the dog's forward movement if he tries to pull. Some (e.g. Pulli, Lupi, Stop-pull) work by pulling up the front legs, thereby taking some of the power out of the dog's front legs. These work well for some dogs, but if you use this type make sure that the harness is not rubbing underneath the dog's legs. Some prolific pullers will rub themselves raw and still not stop pulling – inflicting sores that can easily get infected – so check the area regularly; or better still, have something on the harness (some have a soft material 'sleeve') to stop it rubbing. Others (like the Walkezee) are set up so that as the dog pulls, the chest strap pulls against the chest and top of the leg and slows forward movement. A third type (like the Halti Harness) enables you to 'steer' your dog (using a double-ended lead) in the direction you want to go.

FIXED HARNESSES

These are as they say – harnesses that are put on your dog and the straps stay at a fixed length. The straps are generally adjustable – different makes allow adjustments in different places. The more straps that are adjustable the easier it is to get an exact fit for your dog.

Fixed harnesses will not stop your dog from pulling – indeed, some dogs find it easier to pull in a fixed harness – but it takes the control away from the collar, and if your dog is forever choking on his collar this will help. It is also often recommended for dogs who have neck or back problems as it can take the pressure away from these areas.

It is also essential – for your dog's safety – if you are using a long line or extending lead to attach it to a fixed harness and not to a collar, head collar or training harness.

It is a good idea to use a double-ended lead with a fixed harness (one end on the harness, the other on his collar) so if your dog backs out of it you still have an attachment to his collar.

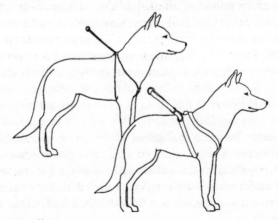

Figure 2.3 Two types of harness.

Leads

It is important to regularly check the condition of your dog's lead.
You will need to check the hook that attaches to the collar as it can
become broken, damaged or jammed with mud, and may cause the
lead to detach from the collar. Also check any stitching, fraying or
areas that the dog may have chewed. If there is anything more than
superficial damage you should replace the lead immediately.

WHAT TYPE OF LEAD?

There are many different types of lead available and individual
preference should be a priority. However, it is important to ensure
that the lead is comfortable to hold and is durable. You may
choose a lead made of leather, rope, or one of the fancy fabric
types. When choosing a lead it is important to consider the dog's
size and strength as a lead that is too thin or has a clip that is too
small could break easily.

Many owners find extending leads helpful when teaching their dog
to come when called, or for dogs that cannot be let off the lead. An
extending lead is a long line, which is contained in the handle, and
the handler controls the length of the lead. While they are ideal for
dogs that are not allowed off the lead they should not be used near
busy roads, as the dog could cause an accident by suddenly walking
into the road or in front of a person. Care must also be taken as
the line can burn the skin if allowed to slip through a person's
hand, or gets caught round your or other people's (or dogs') legs.

DOUBLE-ENDED LEAD

Often called a 'training lead', this useful piece of equipment is
usually about two metres in length, with a G-clip at either end and
several D-rings, which can be used to vary the length of the lead.
It is very useful when used as a double-ended lead with one G-clip
attached to a harness or head collar, and the other to the dog's
flat collar.

INDOOR LINE OR HOUSE LINE

The 'indoor line' or 'house line' facilitates teaching and training. This lightweight line of about two metres is attached to a non-slip collar – one that buckles or fastens and will not tighten up – or fixed harness. It can either be held or allowed to trail behind the dog. The house-line can then be used to remove the dog from unwanted situations. Once new behaviours have become established the line can be removed. However, it can be reintroduced at any time, should the need arise. The line should never be left on a dog that is not being supervised as it can get caught on furniture or doors.

> **Insight**
> All equipment – leads, collars, toys, beds – should be checked regularly for damage, and discarded when necessary.

LONG LINE

A long line is generally from five metres to 15 metres and is attached to the dog's fixed harness enabling it to run free as though off the lead, while allowing the handler/owner reasonable control and facilitating teaching and training. If your dog does not come when called when out on walks and you cannot find an enclosed area to train in, you can attach the long line to his fixed harness. In this way you can practise recalls, but with the safety of an attached line. Do not be tempted to pull him back to you, rather call and reward as if he were off lead. Remember, safety must come first, so take care when using a line and practise using it in your garden or quiet area before using it with distractions around. You should take care that the line does not get caught on people's or other animals' legs as it can cause friction burns and other injuries. With a little practice you can get quite proficient in its use.

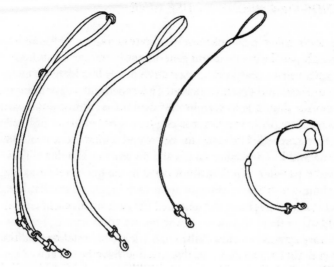

Figure 2.4 Various leads.

Beds

Dogs are by nature denning animals; therefore, ideally your dog should have his own place. Most dogs like somewhere quiet and warm, such as a utility room, kitchen or hallway, but some prefer to be in the middle of the family – perhaps in the living room. Try both types of place and see which he prefers. By providing your dog with his own bed you are giving him refuge; somewhere he can go for some peace and quiet, perhaps to chew a toy or just rest. Puppies, especially, need a lot of sleep. If your puppy (or older dog) is in his bed, ask people to leave him to sleep. Puppies – like children – can easily become overexcited when tired.

When considering what type and size of bed to purchase, ensure you allow sufficient space so that your dog is not cramped or that it is not too big.

TYPES OF BED

Dog beds come in a wide variety of shapes and sizes. Ridged plastic types are resilient and generally suitable for most dogs. Although they can still be chewed, the dog is less likely to chew larger pieces and destroy the bed. This type is also easy to clean. A blanket should be placed in the bottom for comfort and warmth. The most hygienic blankets for dogs are those made of polyester fur fabric, specifically made for dogs, and which are warm, long lasting and less appealing to chew than woollen blankets. This fabric is popular as it is easily washed in the household washing machine. Dogs like to snuggle up in such blankets; smaller breeds tend to like the igloo type, designed for cats, as they can curl up and hide in them. Likewise, beanbags are comfortable, but can be a bit more difficult to clean. Although wicker baskets are traditional they are difficult to clean, and pieces that have been chewed can be swallowed, with dangerous results.

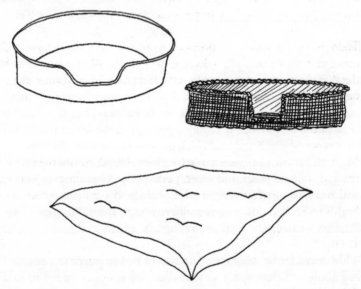

Figure 2.5 Different types of beds.

Brushes

Keeping your dog's coat clean and free from uncomfortable knots and tangles is obviously more important on longer-coated dogs, and usually becomes more time-consuming as the dog becomes older. If you have a long-coated breed that needs professional trimming, or a large breed that you find too time-consuming to bathe, or do not have suitable facilities, consider enlisting the services of a professional groomer. Shop around when looking for a salon; a good groomer will be happy to discuss your dog and his needs and will be willing to spend time getting to know your dog. As well as bathing and trimming your dog, a good salon will clean his ears and cut his nails if necessary. Finding a City and Guilds qualified groomer is always a good idea, as they will have had to trim various breeds to a high standard to achieve this qualification, as well as taking written exams to prove they have a good general knowledge of dog care. Talk to friends and family, or perhaps the staff at your vet's, and try to get a recommendation if possible.

There is a great variety of products available to assist owners with grooming their dogs, and selecting the right brushes and combs for the dog's coat will undoubtedly save time and help produce the best results.

TYPES OF BRUSH

Most owners use a pin or bristle brush on their dog, and the use of this type of brush will benefit most dogs. It acts as a form of massage, which can help improve circulation, muscle tone and promotes healthy skin. It is not, however, effective on knots or tangles.

Insight
Make sure that the type of brush is suitable for your dog.

A bristle brush is ideal for short-coated breeds, to remove dead hair and massage the skin and coat.

Palm pads and rubber hound gloves come in several forms. Palm pads are ideal for Terriers or dogs with wiry coats, whereas the rubber hound glove is more suited to short-coated breeds. Both lift dead hair and dirt from the coat and massage the skin to leave a healthy shine.

The slicker brush comes in many shapes, sizes and strengths and is probably the most used and most useful for long, dense-coated breeds. Although a very effective piece of equipment, if used incorrectly it can cause inflammation and irritation to the skin, so care should be taken when being used.

Moulting combs are available for long- and short-coated dogs and as their name suggests, are designed to remove hair that is ready to moult. The long teeth penetrate the under coat to lift dead hair and the shorter teeth collect it.

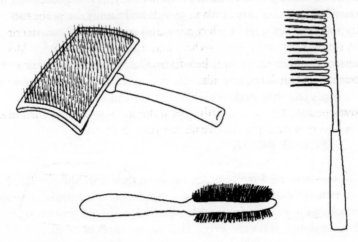

Figure 2.6 Various combs and brushes.

Food and water bowls

A fresh supply of drinking water is essential for all dogs and a shortage can lead to illness. Water is required for various functions in the body, such as the transportation of blood and the elimination of waste.

Never restrict your dog's water intake, unless advised to do so by your vet. Some owners are tempted to restrict water during toilet training but this can be dangerous to your dog.

Insight

Never restrict your dog's water intake unless directed to do so by a veterinary surgeon.

Food and water bowls come in all sorts of shapes, sizes and materials. The choice is down to you, but make sure it is not too big (your dog needs to reach comfortably into the bowl to eat) or too small (food will go everywhere and make a mess). Some older dogs, and some large breeds benefit from a raised bowl. Talk to your vet or breeder about this.

Bowls need to be washed daily. Wash the food bowl after each use. It is best to have separate utensils for your dog's use.

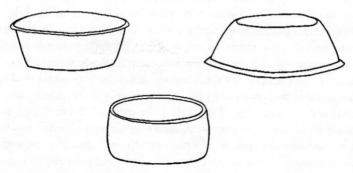

Figure 2.7 Different types of bowls.

Toys

Dogs enjoy games of strength, possession, 'kill' and chase. The type of games your dog will prefer generally depend on what he has been bred for. For example, a Border Collie will enjoy chase games, whereas a Springer Spaniel will enjoy chasing and retrieving.
This is not a rigid rule and dogs can often be encouraged to play 'non-breed-typical' games. Owners can, inadvertently, encourage their dogs to play inappropriate games. For instance, the puppy is bored and notices a tea-towel hanging from its hook. He grabs it – perhaps for a game of tug – and it comes off the hook. The owner notices and lunges at the dog to grab it back. If the owner manages to get hold of it, the puppy gets his game of tug! If the owner doesn't catch it, the puppy runs away with his 'treasure' (it must be important if the owner wants it back). The owner rushes after him and a wonderful (in the puppy's view) game of chase ensues! The puppy has taught his owner a new game called 'chase me, chase me' a game a lot of puppies love. The puppy has learned that a great way of getting attention is to steal something. Not good.

So what should the owner have done? Think back to Chapter 1: Ignore behaviour that you don't like, if you possibly can. Most of us can sacrifice a tea-towel. So when the puppy pulls it from its hook – ignore the behaviour. Chances are that when it lands on the floor the puppy will get bored with it. Even if he doesn't and starts rushing around with it, no great harm is going to be done (it can go into the washing machine after the game). Once he has lost interest, call your puppy to you and start an appropriate game with him – tuggie with a tug toy, fetch, some training or whatever he enjoys – to use up that excess energy. Move the tea-towels so they are not dangling in front of him and gradually re-introduce them to that place when he is less likely to be tempted. A bored puppy needs to have toys to play with, either on his own or with you. In the same way that you would not expect a young child to sit and do nothing all the time, you must be aware that your puppy needs stimulation and interaction with you on a frequent basis.

GAMES DOGS PLAY

The 'killing' game: dogs that play this type of game will shake a rag, soft toy or paper from side to side, shredding it – but they usually lose interest once it is 'dead'. They also play the game with squeaky toys, but again lose all interest after the squeak has been 'killed'. Many dogs will play the game to a certain extent, but Terriers – who were originally bred to catch and kill rats and other rodents – are the real experts at it.

The chase game: most dogs like to play the 'chase game'. Some dogs are obsessed with this game and want to chase anything that moves. Border Collies must be the supreme example of dogs that enjoy the chase game. However, chase games have to be controlled. It is not appropriate for your dog to chase joggers, cyclists, horses or cars.

They should also not be encouraged to chase children, as accidents can happen too easily if the dog gets overexcited (as they often will when playing with children).

Tugging: lots of dogs love to play tug. Keep appropriate toys for tugging – do not fall into the trap of playing tug with anything that your dog brings to you. Also get into the habit of always inviting your dog to 'tug it' before starting the game (whether he initiates or you do). See Chapter 5 for rules on playing tuggie games.

CHEW TOYS

Dogs enjoy chewing. Puppies need to chew, especially when they are teething, and if you don't provide them with appropriate chew toys they will find other things in the house to chew – furniture, carpets, even walls. Chewing can also help puppy to settle down. It helps them to calm down, get rid of stress and to relax enough to sleep. Kongs are strong rubber toys that are super bouncy and irresistible to dogs, especially when stuffed with treats, when they turn into a stimulating food dispenser. Toys that are based on a similar appeal include food cubers and balls, which are toys that the dog can roll or knock around, and have been filled with a selection of treats that are gradually dispensed, keeping the dog amused for long periods. (See Chapter 6 for ideas on stuffing Kongs and similar toys.)

Chew bones might include hard, sterilized bones, which are either empty or pre-filled when purchased; smoked bones or deep-fried marrow bones to softer-basted sinew or rawhide chews. These types of bone are available from pet food suppliers. Do not be tempted to give your dog any bones that you have cooked at home, as they could splinter easily and cause all sorts of problems for your dog. Even with the shop-bought ones you should be vigilant, and ensure that your dog is not able to bite pieces off them, which could be swallowed and cause a blockage. The best type of bones are the ones which turn to powder when your dog chews them. This powder can cause a bit of a mess, so be sure you pet is lying in his bed or on some other washable surface when enjoying his big treat.

Hard rubber toys are available in a variety of colours and assortment of shapes, and although they can be destroyed by constant chewing, they provide hours of stimulation and occupation for lots of dogs.

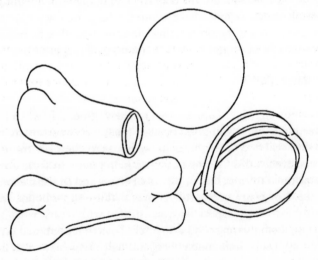

Figure 2.8 A smoked bone and various other hard, rubber toys.

PLAY TOYS

Balls or a ball on a rope are perfect for interactive play or teaching retrieve, because they can be thrown long distances and come in a variety of sizes and colours. For an adult dog who really enjoys the fetching game, you can buy special 'launchers', which allow you to throw the ball a long distance. These are also useful – if your dog hasn't learned to return the ball to your hand – for picking up the ball without having to bend down. Especially useful when playing in a muddy area!

Many dogs like to carry something in their mouth, especially the gun dog breeds. Rope toys are ideal for such dogs, being safe and as well as being a toy, provide useful flossing action during interactive play.

Squeaky toys come in a wide variety of shapes and colours and are generally made of rubber or latex, the former generally lasting a little longer. Many dogs love to squeak the toy until they destroy the squeak mechanism, and then they gradually chew until the toy is unrecognizable. If your dog does chew squeaky toys, be sure to take the 'squeak' away – this is another thing you don't want your dog swallowing.

Take care when choosing any toys that they are an appropriate size for your dog. Too small and your dog could choke on them, too large and he can't carry it. This is particularly true for toys that are going to be used for fetch/retrieve games.

Special 'mind games' for dogs, such as doggy dominoes or solitaire, are available to buy. These games can be quite complex and your dog needs to learn how to win the game and earn his treat. These games should only be used under the supervision of the owner but are a fun and novel way of encouraging your dog to use his brain.

Your dog does not need to have hundreds of toys, but it is nice for him to have a change. So the best thing is to let your dog have some of his toys available, with others tucked away. Every few days swap some of the toys for the ones that have been away for a few days. Check all toys regularly – damaged or torn toys should be replaced.

Figure 2.9 Simple toys including rope and squeaky toy, and complex toys including doggy roulette and solitaire.

Indoor kennel/crate

These can be invaluable when toilet-training your puppy, or when he has to be left alone or unsupervised (as he will need to be). See Chapter 5 about introducing your dog to a crate.

The most popular type of indoor kennel or crate is the fold-down mesh type. They come in a variety of sizes and because they collapse they can be easily transported. The crate is a wonderful training aid if introduced and used correctly.

The crate should be long enough for the dog to turn around in and stretch, also high enough for him to sit up without touching the top. Ideally, the crate should be placed in an area close to the family. Positioning it in a corner, with a sheet or towel covering the top and sides, gives the dog a cosy, secure, 'den' feeling.

A crate can be used when you cannot supervise your puppy, which will mean that your puppy will not get into mischief. A crate can be a big help with house-training as no dog likes to mess his bed and is likely to cry to be let out to go to the toilet. What it is *not* is a 'sin bin' where puppies are put for hours at a time.

If your puppy is in his crate overnight, or for any length of time during the day, make sure he has newspaper in the crate, away from his bedding, which he can use if he needs to toilet and you are not there to let him out.

Do not leave a collar on your puppy when he is alone and in his crate, as it can get caught on the bars.

10 THINGS TO REMEMBER

1 By law your dog must wear an identity tag, with your name and address on it. A telephone number is optional, but very useful.

2 Do not use an extendable lead near a road.

3 Regularly check collars and leads for damage and wear.

4 Take time and care when introducing head collars or a harness. You should not expect your dog to accept something new straight away.

5 Make sure the brush or comb you are using to groom your dog is suitable for his coat type.

6 Ensure your dog has a comfortable bed in which he can relax.

7 Make sure your dog has access to clean water at all times.

8 Have a selection of safe toys for your dog – some that you can use to play a game with him, and some that he can use to amuse himself.

9 Kongs and similar toys can be stuffed with your dog's dinner and will occupy him for a lot longer than just eating it from a bowl.

10 Crates can be very useful, especially for puppies, but take care when introducing it to your dog and never use it for punishment.

3

Socialization

In this chapter you will learn:
- *what socialization is*
- *how to socialize your puppy effectively*
- *how to handle and groom your dog effectively.*

What is socialization? Socialization is a term that is often misunderstood. It does not mean that a dog is going to learn how to romp and play with other dogs, but rather a term that means getting a dog used to the world it will live in.

Insight
Socialization and habituation are two of the most important things you can do for your puppy.

Many owners who are told 'make sure your puppy is socialized' imagine that they just need to find a bunch of puppies for their own puppy to play with. But socializing is much more than this. Socialization is perhaps best described as the process whereby an animal learns how to recognize and interact with the species with which it cohabits. In other words, how to behave around people, other dogs, cats, perhaps chickens, horses – any animals that it might come into contact with. The other part of this is technically termed 'habituation', and this can be defined as your dog getting accustomed to non-threatening environmental stimuli – traffic, shiny floors, black bin-bags – and learning to ignore them.

Because dogs need to learn about and accept the natural world around them and not be scared by things they will come across in their daily lives, they have an inborn period of time called the socialization period. This is a finite time when puppies will be curious and willing to investigate novel things. The time occurs between three and five months, with easy socializing and habituation ending at about four and a half months depending on breed and personality. You need to expose your puppy to as many things in its environment as possible. If your puppy has not had his vaccinations, it is still possible to socialize him. Ask friends with dogs who are well socialized, have nice temperaments and are fully vaccinated to come round to your house and garden so that your puppy can interact with other dogs; ask different friends of all ages to visit and have positive interactions with your puppy; take him for short journeys in the car.

Your puppy's experiences should be positive, using play and treats to form an association with all the things he will encounter throughout his life. These include car rides, the vet's surgery, skateboards, bikes, traffic, children of all ages, men, women, horses; in fact, the list is endless and will depend to some extent on where you live, your lifestyle and where your puppy is likely to go over the next 14 years or so. If, for instance, you like to ride and spend a lot of time at the stables it is important for your puppy to meet horses. If, on the other hand, you live in the middle of a big city and never step foot in the countryside it is important for him to get used to trucks and buses, but perhaps less important for him to meet cows.

It is very important for him to meet lots of people – even if you rarely go out sooner or later he is at least going to have to deal with people at the vet's surgery, or those who come to the house. But for most of us, taking our dog to the park or walks through the town is part of the joy of owning a dog. You may want to take your dog when you visit friends, or have friends round without the dog being scared.

Remember how specific a dog is – you may think a child is a child, but to a dog a toddler is very different from a six-year-old child, and both of these are very different from a teenager. So they need to have good, safe interactions with children of all ages (always supervised), with different people – to a puppy, a man with a beard is different from a clean-shaven man. Hats, gloves, sunglasses, walking sticks, umbrellas – all these things make a person look different, especially to your dog. So it is no good introducing your dog to half a dozen people and a couple of five-year-olds and think you have socialized him to people – you haven't.

Insight

Your puppy needs to meet all types of people, safe dogs and other animals as soon as possible.

Your puppy needs to interact with as many puppies and older dogs as possible. But these interactions must be positive or you will be doing the opposite of what you want to achieve. If your puppy meets lots of dogs who bully him, he will learn to be scared of other dogs. This may well turn into aggression when he is older – he will feel that he has to keep other dogs away. It is also not good if he finds out that he can bully other puppies, as he will become the 'thug' in the park that everyone tries to avoid! Not all adult dogs enjoy the company of puppies, so before letting him approach another dog, check with the owner that their dog is happy to greet him. Puppies can be very 'in your face' and some dogs do not like this. If you have your puppy off lead and see an owner putting their dog on lead, this is a signal that you should heed. It may mean that the other dog has a poor recall, so its owner doesn't want to risk him coming to your dog and not being able to get him back, but it may mean – and often does – that the dog is not good around other dogs. So, if you see a dog going on lead, call your puppy to you, and do not let him approach the other dog unless he is invited to do so by the other owner.

You should always have respect for a dog on a lead. If he is on lead he has no choice about meeting an incoming dog; he cannot run away or hide if he is frightened. If your puppy/dog is on lead and so is the other dog (perhaps you are walking near a road), check whether the other dog will be comfortable for yours to approach.

If he is, let them say hello in a controlled manner, but be very careful that you do not tangle leads. It can be very scary for a dog to feel he is trapped against another dog, and it would not be a positive experience for either of them. If the other dog backs off, do not allow your puppy/dog to follow him. The dog is backing off because he is scared or cautious, so give him time to decide whether he wants to interact with your puppy/dog – he may not be as well socialized as yours. If he comes back to your dog then the meeting can continue, but if not then do the kind thing and keep your puppy/dog away.

Below is a list – and you can add to it many more things that are relevant to your lifestyle – which you should strive to introduce to your puppy before he is 18 weeks old. It is quite a tall order, but well worth the effort.

cars		men/hat		tarmac		playground	
bikes		men/tall		mud		pensioners	
tractors		men/short		sand		motorbikes	
lorries		women/umbrella		pebbles		bus	
buses		women/tall		lakes		trains	
roads		women/short		the sea		escalators	
vans		women/glasses		prams		markets	
horses/rider		children		pushchairs		fairground	
sheep		bikes		babies			
cows		balls		toddlers			
dogs		skipping		geese			
cats		running		ducks			
men		skateboards		swans			
women		gates		country lane			
children		stiles		busy road			
men/beards		car parks		bridges			
men/glasses		wheelchairs		town centre			
men/umbrella		grass		schools			

It is well worth the time and trouble to fit in as many different environmental elements as possible. Make a chart so that you can check how many different things your puppy has encountered. This chart is just to get you started. The more things you add, the better socialized your dog will be.

You can never cover all eventualities but if you think about it logically, what you are teaching your puppy during this period is to view novel experiences as pleasurable.

Handling your puppy is very important (see section on 'Handling and grooming' below). Your puppy needs to learn that being touched and held is a rewarding experience. Not only will you have to handle your puppy to groom him, to dry his feet and maybe take out the odd tick or two, but there are many other people who will have to handle your puppy throughout his life such as the veterinary surgeon and the groomer, to name but two. Ask family and friends whom your puppy knows well to handle and hand feed your puppy by sitting on the floor, feeding small tasty treats as they look into his ears, hold onto his paws and feel down his legs and under his tummy.

If your puppy is a shy reserved type, make sure that you allow the interaction to be at his own pace and do not force him to take food. You should always supervise this handling to make sure that your puppy is safe.

Socialization may seem an unnecessary and boring part of your puppy's training, but it is critical. The more interesting and pleasurable puppyhood experiences your dog can dip into in later life, the more resilient and stable its character will be.

Occasionally something can go wrong and your puppy will view the experience as frightening. Whatever the bad experience, it must be addressed sensibly and unemotionally. You need to re-establish that the element is safe and pleasant.

One of the more common problems encountered is when another dog or puppy is overly aggressive. If your puppy has been frightened by the encounter it is imperative that he is introduced to gentle, safe and sociable dogs as soon after his frightening experience as possible. Your puppy should be allowed to interact with this type of dog at his own pace, allowing him to learn that other dogs are not threatening. If you are unsure about finding the right type of dog to reintroduce your puppy to, contact your local APDT trainer and ask if they can help.

Puppy classes

Choose your puppy class carefully!

A qualified and knowledgeable trainer should supervise any puppy-to-puppy play. They will understand the importance of having puppies of similar temperament playing together and what harm can be done if some simple order is not adhered to!

All training in a good puppy class should use positive reinforcement. This means teaching your puppy by rewarding the behaviour you like, rather than punishing the behaviour you do not like.

All APDT trainers use positive reinforcement methods and can easily be contacted by going to the website www.apdt.co.uk or contacting your local vet.

The older puppy or adult dog

If you have taken on an older dog, this does not mean it cannot be socialized. It just takes longer, and sometimes you may find that the dog has already built up some bad associations. As with a puppy, introduce your dog to as many people and environmental elements as possible, associating each one with a rewarding experience.

Note: If your dog is showing any fearful, worried or aggressive behaviour, you might need the help of a behaviourist. Such behaviour can be addressed but needs a specialized plan of action for the individual dog. Ask your vet for a referral, as a dog should always be checked for health problems which may be causing the problem, before seeing a behaviourist. A good behaviourist will always ask you to do this before a consultation.

Dog-to-dog socialization

Under-socialized dogs will not necessarily be fearful around other dogs. They may well be interested in other dogs but just lack social greeting skills. Many puppies or adolescent dogs are way over the top when greeting other dogs, and can annoy older dogs with their crude and often boisterous body language.

The best way of teaching these dogs how to interact with their own kind is to give them regular contact with well-socialized adult dogs. These dogs will not tolerate too much crude behaviour but will do no harm when showing the younger dog how to behave. The very worst you can do with these young under-skilled dogs is to keep them away from other dogs. If they are not allowed to learn the correct greeting manoeuvres, valuable social lessons will never be learned. Training during this period is crucial. We all want dogs that socialize well with their own species but not at the expense of ignoring their owners. Dogs and puppies need to learn how to walk past another dog without interacting with it.

▶ *With your dog on a flat collar and lead, ask him to sit as another dog approaches.*
▶ *Keep a reasonable distance between the two dogs and reward your dog as he sits and the other dog walks past.*
▶ *Be generous with your rewards at this stage and keep your dog's attention on you. As long as your dog remains in a sit, reward with small tasty treats.*

- *Use the same technique to teach your dog to walk politely past another dog.*
- *As the unknown dog approaches, have a handful of small rewards ready and attract your dog's attention by saying his name and a cue to 'look'.*
- *When your dog pays attention to you, give a reward.*
- *Keep doing this as the other dog walks past.*

If you think about this from your dog's point of view, you are teaching him the habit of automatically looking to you when another dog approaches. As the habit of training becomes ingrained you can reward your dog at less frequent intervals. There will be times when you will allow your dog to interact with other dogs, but using this technique you will have a dog that will look to you for permission to interact with a strange dog.

Teach your dog that there are different signals or cues when another dog approaches.

- *The signal of look or listen means pay attention to you and ignore the other dog.*
- *The signal of 'say hello' or something similar means you can interact with the other dog.*

When your dog is off lead and playing with another dog you will need to know how to regain his attention.

Read the section in Chapter 6 on recall training.

Handling and grooming

All dogs must learn how to cope with being handled. This may be for grooming purposes, for veterinary treatment or simply being petted. Some dogs love being touched and will actively crave attention by pushing their muzzle under a hand or pawing at you. Others dislike or are indifferent about physical contact. This does not make one type of dog better than the other, just different!

Learning to enjoy human handling is imperative and your reward for taking the time and trouble to teach your dog these lessons will be a dog that other people find a pleasure.

The best way to teach your dog how to enjoy being handled is to associate handling with something pleasant.

Insight
Associate handling with something pleasant.

Whether your dog is long-or short-coated, they all need to be brushed. Not only will this keep your dog's coat and skin in good condition but will also help you spot any abnormalities such as lumps or skin irritations.

Most dogs find different parts of their body more sensitive than others. With some it may be the tail, others behind the ears or maybe their paws. If your dog shows a dislike of having a particular part of his body being touched, do not avoid this area, but rather pay special attention to associating it with a rewarding experience. This is especially important around the tail region, as that is where the vet will put a thermometer if your dog needs to have his temperature taken.

INTRODUCING STAGES OF GROOMING

Before we start, let's think about what we want the dog to learn. We want the dog not just to tolerate grooming but actually enjoy the experience. The easiest way to teach this is to exploit the way a dog learns.

Dogs spend their time watching for signals that will affect their lives. A signal can mean something good is going to happen or something bad.

A lead usually signals a good thing is going to happen, a walk!
A tin opener might signal that dinner is on its way!
A hand near the dog should signal cuddles, fuss, food or toys!

A brush can signal a bad thing is about to happen – having your hair pulled. Nail clippers can signal restraint and, if done badly, pain! Hands can signal punishment or maybe denial of something.

We need to teach the dog that hands, brushes, nail clippers and so on are signals that something good is going to happen.

INTRODUCING GROOMING SIGNALS

Run your hand gently along your dog's body and then give your dog a tasty treat. Teach your dog that every time your hand appears and touches him, it is a signal that something good is going to happen. Repeat this until your dog is showing you he is looking forward to being touched. Your aim is for your dog to enjoy being touched all over. As I mentioned at the beginning, some dogs will find this an easy exercise and others may take a little longer. When your dog is happy being handled it is time to introduce a brush.

Insight
Take your time about introducing grooming to your dog.

Produce the brush and then give your dog a treat. Repeat this until your dog is obviously enjoying the brush appearing. Move on to touching your dog with the brush and then feeding a very tasty treat. When your dog is actively showing you that being touched by the brush is something he is looking forward to, go on to the next stage of actually brushing your dog. Start with short sessions, perhaps brushing different parts of your dog at each session. Remember to give your dog an interesting treat each time you brush him. Using the same technique:

1 *Check his paws and between the toes. Dogs will often pick up grass seeds and these must be removed.*
2 *When your dog is happy to have his paws held, introduce the nail clippers. Do this in exactly the same way using the clippers to signal something good is going to happen.*
3 *Space this over as many sessions as is necessary for your dog to feel happy when the clippers are produced. Move on to touching your dog's claws with the clippers.*

4 When your dog is responding in a way that tells you he likes
   the clippers to touch his nails, cut just one nail per session
   using the same signalling technique. Never cut below the quick,
   for just like us this is very painful and will bleed profusely. If
   you are in any doubt about how much you can trim, ask your
   vet when you take your puppy for his vaccinations.

5 Teeth must be kept clean and checked often. This is done by
   giving your dog a word or cue such as 'open', opening his
   mouth gently and popping in a food treat. Your dog should
   soon learn to associate the word 'open' with opening his mouth.

6 To clean your dog's teeth, take a small amount of dog
   toothpaste, place it on your finger and rub it around the gums
   and teeth. After a few sessions of this you can progress to a
   small-headed toothbrush and gently brush your dog's teeth.

7 If you keep up with this routine two or three times a week
   throughout your dog's life you will keep your dog's teeth
   healthy.

8 Ears and eyes need to be kept free of foreign bodies, so you
   need to teach your dog to enjoy having these checked. Ears
   should have a pleasant odour. If your dog's ears have an
   unpleasant smell it is an indication that he has an infection
   and must be taken to the vet immediately.

Your dog may show signs of not wishing to have parts of his
body handled. This can take the form of keeping very still and
growling or perhaps wriggling and biting. Never punish your dog
for displaying this type of behaviour. He is using the only way
he knows to tell you not to touch this area. Take your dog to the
vet and make sure that he is physically well. If your dog is fit and
well but still displaying these signs, it is because past experience
has taught him that growling or biting has the desired effect, e.g.
humans back away. Contact your nearest member of the APDT
who will either help you sort the problem out without punishment,
or will be able to refer you to the nearest qualified behaviour
counsellor, and they will help you understand and correct the
undesired behaviour.

Remember, grooming and handling your dog should be a pleasant
experience for both of you.

10 THINGS TO REMEMBER

1 It is important for your puppy to be introduced to as many different types of people as possible.

2 Your puppy should have the opportunity to meet safe adult dogs as well as meeting puppies of a similar age.

3 Acclimatize your puppy to the noises inside (washing machine, hairdryer, vacuum cleaner) and outside (traffic, aeroplanes, dustbins being moved) your home.

4 Do not increase your puppy's fear of unknown objects by inadvertently reinforcing fearful reactions.

5 If he is unsure of something or someone, let him take his time to get used to them. Do not force him to approach – this will make things worse, not better.

6 Take your puppy to as many different places as you can – the station, the market, the bank – anywhere that your puppy is allowed into.

7 If you have taken on an older dog it is still important to socialize him, so make sure he is happy to be around people and other animals.

8 Get your puppy used to being handled so he is happy for you to check his feet, eyes, ears etc.

9 Get your puppy/dog used to travelling by car, bus, or train as early as possible. Ensure that the majority of his journeys are to enjoyable places like the park, or a friend's house, and only some of them are to places which are not so much fun like the vet's or groomer's.

10 Take care when choosing a training class for your dog. Do not go to a class just because it is close to your home.

4

Before you begin

In this chapter you will learn:
- *how to decide what you want from your dog*
- *about the right words to use*
- *how to get the family on track.*

Taking on a puppy is a big responsibility. He may be a member of your family for the next 14 or 15 years, so you need to start the way you mean to carry on. There are two key points to consider before training begins, or even before you get your puppy.

1 *What you want or don't want your adult dog to do in the house.*
2 *What you want or don't want your adult dog to do in the way of obedience inside or outside.*

Indoors

Chapter 5 looks at 'Puppy issues' and explains how to train your dog to be a well-behaved member of your family while in the house. Therefore, the first thing you must do as a family is to decide what will be acceptable for your dog to do indoors and what won't.

Insight
Decide what the rules will be for your puppy/dog.

Before you get your puppy, sit down as a family and write a list of things that you are happy for your puppy to do indoors and those that you will not be quite so happy with. Then, beside each of those items write a 'cue word' that you will use when teaching your puppy, for each of those items. When using cue words, the entire family must be consistent in their use. If someone in the family uses a different word, then it will only confuse your puppy and make the training process longer. For example, the first thing you are likely to teach a puppy is to go to the toilet outside, so you will need a cue for this – 'be clean' is a common one to use, but it must be consistent if your puppy is to learn in the shortest possible time. As he becomes more accustomed to toileting outside, the cue can be used to let your pup know what you are expecting of him. (See the 'House-training' section in Chapter 5.)

Alternatively, you may not want your adult dog lying on your sofa, so firstly do not encourage him onto the sofa when he is still a puppy, or if you would like him on the sofa sometimes but not others you still need to teach a cue to invite him up and another to ask him to get off.

Insight

Decide what your cue words will be.

You may not want your puppy to go into certain rooms; the baby's bedroom, for example. Baby-gates are really useful to block off rooms where your dog is not allowed without having to shut him out altogether. So fit your baby-gates before your puppy arrives home so that you start as you mean to go on.

Having decided on your list and cue words, write them down and attach them to the fridge door or the family notice board so if at any time someone forgets what a cue is, they can easily refer to it.

Outdoors

Similarly, you will need to decide as a family what you would like your dog to do in the way of basic 'obedience'. Chapter 6 describes a number of things that most pet dog owners would like their dog to do, but just as teaching what is and isn't acceptable indoors, your dog will need to be taught a cue for each exercise. Depending on your experiences with dogs, you might find teaching the right behaviours to have a well-behaved sociable dog is sufficient. On the other hand, you might like to be a little more adventurous and teach more advanced exercises. Whatever you require from your dog, decide on a cue for each behaviour; again, write a list of each behaviour and write the cue next to it so everyone in the family uses the same word and hand signal for the same behaviour.

Once you have a list of what you want to teach your puppy and the cue for each exercise, then attach them to the fridge door or notice board.

A word about words

It's important to think about the words you will be using as cues so as not to confuse your puppy.

One of the first things your puppy will need to learn is his name. When to use his name and when not to use his name is very important. Primarily you should use your puppy's name to get his attention. Once you have his attention you can then give him a cue, and while you have his attention, you needn't repeat it every time you ask him to do something. For example, if you want your puppy to do a sequence of sit, stay, come to you, and sit, you would say his name initially to get his attention, then the cues for each exercise individually. A common mistake is to go through this sequence by saying. 'Rover sit; Rover stay; Rover come; Rover sit.' What you will end up with is words where the puppy's name and the cue join together and end up as 'roversit, roverstay, rovercome, roversit' and your puppy's name will eventually become meaningless.

Also avoid using your puppy's name as a cue to call him back to you. Your puppy will hear his name mentioned probably dozens of times a day. You will use it to get his attention; you'll probably talk to him and use his name, 'Good boy, Rover' for example. You may have conversations with friends or neighbours where his name is mentioned; he may not react but he will hear it. For this reason, it can be very confusing for your puppy to know whether he is needed to do something or not whenever he hears his name.

Words that sound the same but have different meanings can be confusing. For example, if you use the word 'heel' to teach your puppy to walk nicely beside you on the lead, and the word 'here' to get him to come back to you, the two words sound similar and can therefore confuse your puppy. So try to think of words that are very clear and dissimilar.

It's very easy to use human terminology on our dogs and expect them to understand. How many times is the term 'sit down' used to get people, well, to sit down? It's very common to use the word 'sit' to teach a puppy to sit, and 'down' to get him to lie down. If you use these words for those exercises, then saying, 'sit down' to your puppy is only going to confuse him. 'Do they want me to sit or lie down?' So use 'sit' for sit and 'down' for lie down. Alternatively, if you want to use 'sit down' when teaching your puppy to sit, you will need to think of another cue when teaching him to lie down; 'flat', for example.

It's also very easy but unwise to use a word that means several different actions. The word 'down' is a good example. 'Down' can mean 'lie down', 'get off the furniture', and 'stop jumping up at me'. That is one word for three different actions. When making your list of what you want to teach your puppy, whether indoors or outdoors, think of cues that are unique to a particular exercise or command so you have one word meaning one thing. The actual words are not overly important – if you decide that 'clock' means 'sit' and 'chair' means 'lie down' the cues will still work if everyone uses the same word – but it makes sense to use words that will come easily to everyone who interacts with your dog. You could make all your cues Italian, or French, for it makes no difference to your dog. Until the words are associated with a reward they will mean nothing to him. He doesn't understand words in any human language until he is taught them by association.

Motivation

You are also going to have to find out what motivates your puppy. With many dogs, particularly puppies, food is a great motivator, but you will need to find out what food motivates him more than anything else. You will need to find several different foods and grade them as to how much he values them. A piece of kibble (dry dog food) that he is fed for his meals three or four times a day may motivate him, but only for so long. A piece of frankfurter on the other hand may be a high grade of motivator! You will need to grade the rewards as the training progresses when you have found several foods that motivate your puppy. Another list for the notice board! An example of a list of rewards or motivators might be, at the bottom kibble, next up a dog biscuit, above that a dog treat, above that cheese, above that sausage and top of the list is livercake. This is only one example – your dog might have a game with a tuggie or ball at the top of the list. The list may change sometimes. But at all times make sure it is *your dog's* idea of reward, and not *yours*.

When training your dog, try to use the lower graded rewards first, especially if you are working at home with no distractions. If your dog is not particularly 'foody' you will need to work with a higher grade. When you are working with more distractions – someone else is in the house, perhaps, or you are in the garden and there are smells and sights to distract your dog – then you should use a higher grade. When you are at the park and there are numerous distractions, then you will need to work with very high-grade rewards initially. Keep a regular check on your puppy's weight during the early training and make adjustments to his daily food intake if necessary.

Other pups are motivated by toys, but again you must find several toys that will motivate him, and then grade them; so you start with a low grade toy and know what his favourite game is for when he's done really well or you are working with lots of distractions.

You will find that as you progress with training, some things will motivate your puppy indoors while others will be more motivating outdoors. The higher the distraction the higher the reward. It's just a question of experimenting and finding out what your puppy really likes rather than what you think he likes.

Older dogs

If you acquire an older dog from a re-homing centre, you may find that he is trained to a certain degree. In which case, the re-homing staff may be able to provide you with a list of cues the dog understands. If your dog is comfortable with these cues, carry on using them. Sometimes however, a cue can have bad associations; 'in your bed' is a classic example. If the dog has come from a family where going to bed is a punishment he is not going to be comfortable hearing his old cue, so change it. Teach him that going to his bed is a good thing (there are toys and perhaps a stuffed Kong there) and introduce a new cue – 'have a rest', perhaps.

If your new dog is not trained, you will have to start from scratch as with a puppy (described above).

There is a risk, however, that if your dog has not been trained he may very well have some 'bad habits', so these will have to be addressed while you are training your dog. If, for example, he has learned that running away when called is more rewarding than coming back you will need to teach a recall from basics, with plenty of high-grade rewards when he returns, and lots of patience when he doesn't. The principle of thinking about what you want your dog to do, or not to do, being consistent with the cues and finding out what motivates him are the same as with a puppy. For more information about re-homed dogs, please refer to 'Taking it further'.

10 THINGS TO REMEMBER

1 *How many children has your dog met?*

2 *Have you taken your dog to the railway station?*

3 *Has your dog met a person with an umbrella?*

4 *Is your dog comfortable with having his ears, eyes and teeth looked at?*

5 *Has your dog met a cat?*

6 *Will your dog stay in the room when you switch the vacuum cleaner on?*

7 *How many puppies has your dog played with?*

8 *How many safe adult dogs has your puppy met?*

9 *Does your dog stand still when you dry him after a walk in the rain?*

10 *Is your dog comfortable when you are near traffic?*

Puppy issues

In this chapter you will learn:
* *how to house-train your puppy*
* *how to deal with 'puppy biting'*
* *how to prevent problem behaviours.*

The importance of play

Puppies need to learn how to relate to their own species – how to read body signals, how to use body language to deflect aggressive displays, how to invite play with other dogs, how to build a relationship with us as their owners – and they do all this through play.

Through playing with a variety of dogs and puppies your pet will learn the importance of having a soft mouth (see 'Play biting' below), effective use of body language and how to deal with dogs of all shapes and sizes. Through playing with you, his owner, he will learn the basis of a good relationship, all manner of cues, how to have self-control, how to wait for something he wants, and most importantly of all how to have fun with you and others.

Rather than always walking round the park chatting to other dog owners, and ignoring your dog, remember to frequently call him back for a treat or a game, maybe even put him on the lead for a minute or two and then release him to 'go play'. This will not only improve your relationship, but it will avoid him staying away from you when you call him in at the end of the walk. Quite often, especially with a young dog, if you aren't paying attention to him he can learn to play inappropriately or roughly with other dogs, perhaps bullying them or being bullied by them. This could lead to behavioural issues later in life.

Appropriate controlled play can help build the confidence of a shy dog, and a boisterous dog can learn self-control if you teach him how to wait for what he wants.

Appropriate games

There are many games that we can play with our puppy, and as owners we should actively encourage and enjoy them, but some games are wholly inappropriate and can lead to a great deal of trouble when your puppy becomes a fully grown dog. Rough and tumble games are a great favourite when your puppy is small, especially with the men and children in the house, but these kind of games will quickly escalate out of control because the puppy learns that biting people is OK, and you could be heading for disaster. Play games that you can all enjoy.

Hide and seek around the garden can also help with recalls. Hold onto your puppy and send one of your children to hide (initially in a very obvious place), then get the puppy to 'go find'. Your child could help by calling the puppy's name. As soon as the puppy gets there the child should give him a treat. You can also hide a biscuit or a toy and send the puppy to find it. Start by letting your puppy see where you are putting it and once he has the idea, gradually make it a bit more difficult for him.

Fetch, where your dog brings back a ball or toy. Make sure that the ball is a suitable size for your puppy, too small and he may choke on it, too large and he will not be able to hold it.

Tuggie: despite outdated thinking, appropriately controlled games of tuggie are a good way of improving your relationship with your puppy, and gives you another reward to use in training. Wiggle the tuggie toy on the floor and wait for your puppy to pounce on it. As he does, invite him to 'tug it'. Play for a short time (ten seconds or so) then show him a small tasty treat. He will probably spit out the tuggie to take the treat. As he spits it out say 'leave' or 'off', give him the treat, and then start playing again by repeating the above. It is important that your puppy wins this game sometimes, and if he wants to run off with the toy, that is also fine. But take care when playing tuggie with a puppy or dog with poor teeth or gums.

A shy puppy can improve his confidence by winning often.

Training games: get your children to help you with training the puppy (see Chapter 6) as it's a great way for them to build up a trusting relationship. If the training is fun for you and them, it will certainly be fun for your puppy.

Children (particularly very young ones) should always be supervised when working, playing or just being with a puppy or dog.

Safety should be the first consideration when teaching a game to a puppy or dog. Encouraging herding breeds to chase, for example, may well lead to them chasing joggers or cyclists in the park. Bull breeds enjoy rough and tumble games, but these can easily get out of control so should not be encouraged in even young dogs.

House-training

The time it takes to house-train your puppy will depend on several things, not least on how vigilant you are. It can also depend on his size, as larger dogs tend to be quicker to house-train – they have larger bladders and so can hold on to their urine longer through the night – and whether your breeder has started house-training him before you bring him home. It can also depend on the diet that you feed. If you feed a dried diet your dog will need to drink more and so wee more. However, you should not restrict the amount of water your puppy drinks, as this can cause serious health problems; if you feed a cheaper diet that has bulk added there is more waste, and your dog will need to poo more.

If you use newspaper or puppy pads indoors to house-train your puppy, you are environmentally teaching him that it is OK to go inside the house; and soon you will have to change this and teach him that you would like him to go to the toilet outside. So house-training can take double the amount of time. If you do use newspaper, how will he know the difference between the newspaper you have put in the kitchen and the paper that you hadn't finished reading yet that you put on the floor near the sofa? If you live in a home with no private garden, and have to train him in the house (until he is allowed to go on the ground in public places) you may find that a piece of turf, placed in a litter tray or plant tray, is more useful. He will then associate grass with going to the toilet.

Most puppies give many clues that they are just about to 'go'; they may sniff the floor and circle, they may become agitated and move around while they are looking for somewhere to go, they may whine or move towards the door and you may miss it, only finding the puddle on the floor later on.

Generally puppies will need to toilet when they wake up, or not long after they have eaten, or after a good play time, and more or less every one to two hours, until they are several months old. Take your puppy outside and let him wander around and sniff, perhaps play with him for a couple of minutes and then allow him to go and sniff. It is important that you stay outside with him or he will be tempted to go back into the house before he has toileted. Let him begin to go to the toilet before you say 'be clean' (or whatever you want your cue word to be) as he may stop what he is doing and come to you. When he has finished going to the toilet, reward him with a small treat. Don't take him inside to give him a treat because you will be rewarding him for going back into the house. Take a small treat with you outside and reward him as soon as he has finished. Most puppies are very food-motivated and you will find your house-training will be a great deal quicker if you reward him every time he goes to the toilet outside.

If your puppy has an accident inside the house and you don't see him, just clean it up with cleaner specifically for the job (your local pet shop sells lots of it). If you use household disinfectant or bleach it will only mask the smell from your nose for a short while. Your puppy has a much better sense of smell than you have, and will sniff around the carpet, and smelling old urine and ammonia will stimulate him to go on that spot again. If you do catch him in the middle of going to the toilet inside the house, make a sound to distract him (e.g. clap your hands) and take him outside as quickly as possible. Don't punish him, or you will teach him that going to the toilet when you are around is not nice, and so even if you are outside he will not want to go to the toilet while you are there. House-training takes time and consistency, so if you need to leave your puppy for more than two hours, ask someone to call in and let him out to go to the toilet. Crates are a useful aid to house-training (see Chapters 2 and 7).

Insight

House-training takes time, patience and consistency.

Play biting

Puppy owners are often concerned that they have an aggressive puppy when their puppy is jumping up and biting them. This is natural behaviour for a puppy and how they play with their litter mates. It gives them the opportunity to learn just how hard they shouldn't bite!

Insight

Play biting is a natural puppy behaviour.

When your puppy arrives at your home he has no more litter mates to play with and so he will play with you, and the way puppies play is by using their teeth. Puppies will also bite a bit more when they begin to lose their puppy teeth, and it is important that they are given something suitable to chew to relieve their teeth and gums. There are lots of puppy toys that you can give him, but do be careful with soft plastic toys which can easily be chewed to pieces in a matter of minutes.

Whenever you give your puppy a new toy, watch him with it for a couple of minutes to make sure that it can withstand your puppy's teeth. Rope tuggie toys are something that they can get their teeth into, and you could also freeze a carrot for your puppy to chew; the coldness should ease his gums if they are sore from teething. Cardboard boxes, after ensuring all staples have been removed, are good as disposable toys. Yes, they make a mess, but it's better than the mess your puppy could make of the furniture, and boxes can be replaced easily. You can fill a small cardboard box with scrunched up newspaper and hide biscuits in it, to give him some fun, and keep his teeth off your skin for a while. Puppies usually grow out of play biting by the time they are about 20 weeks, but bite inhibition is an important lesson your puppy learns from you while he is still using his teeth.

Bite inhibition

Puppy teeth are needle sharp and can be very painful. Teaching bite inhibition is all about teaching your puppy just how hard his bite is and teaching him to have a soft mouth. It teaches your puppy how to use his mouth gently.

Insight
Bite inhibition teaches your dog to use his mouth gently.

Accidents happen. Your child might ride over your dog's tail with his bike; you may come home drunk on New Year's Day and fall over your dog. If you hurt your dog his only defence is to use his mouth and teeth. If he ever gets in the position where he feels he has to bite, and he has good bite inhibition, then damage should be minimal. Every dog can bite. If frightened, in pain or threatened, your dog might bite. That doesn't in any way make him a bad dog. It makes him a dog! You need to teach your dog that human skin is incredibly fragile.

Teaching bite inhibition is divided into four stages. The first two stages are all about making the bites softer, and the second two stages are about decreasing the frequency of bites. The training must be done in this order because if you decrease the frequency first your dog won't learn to soften his bite.

▶ Stage 1 *No painful bites. Ninety per cent of puppies will stop biting you if you give a loud high-pitched yelp. If your puppy backs off, praise and reinforce by continuing your game. The other ten per cent of puppies who just bite harder and get more excited by your loud, high-pitched yelp are usually overtired, overstimulated or belong to the terrier breeds. If this is your puppy then you need to end any interactions as soon as your puppy begins to bite by getting up and walking away for a couple of minutes. This is punishment enough; after all, your puppy is just being a puppy. If you end the interaction you need to get away from your puppy with as little fuss or attention as possible. Even negative attention is attention. Or, have a baby-gate up so you can move yourself totally out of the area. Puppy teeth do hurt and can make you bleed, but you do need to have patience with this. Puppy mouthing is perfectly natural behaviour and we are simply teaching them to be gentle with their mouth.*
▶ Stage 2 *You need to teach your puppy to use less pressure. He needs to understand that his bite is painful. If he bites, yelp and look at your hand as if it is really painful, while stopping interaction with him for a few seconds. (This is what would happen if he was playing with his litter mates and bit too hard.) Next time he starts to bite it should not be as hard. Gradually set your limit softer and softer.*
▶ Stage 3 *It is OK for your puppy to 'mouth' you in play, but any hard bites still interrupt the game/interaction.*

▶ Stage 4 *Finally your puppy needs to learn that he must never initiate biting or 'mouthing' (not using his teeth). So any kind of mouthing stops the game or interaction with him.*

None of these stages requires anything more punishing than time-outs or withdrawal of attention. When teaching these behaviours put your hands in your dog's mouth all the time. Get him used to your being there. Make sure you can open his mouth and examine his teeth, because the vet is going to do it, and you should prepare your puppy for it.

Chewing

Puppies chew for various reasons, such as boredom, teething, exploring things with their mouth; and it is up to us to teach them what is acceptable to chew and what is not. All puppies chew as they begin to lose their teeth at around the age of four months. They begin another teething stage when they reach about eight months as their teeth set into their jaw. Both stages are a necessary part of puppy development and some breeds of dog excel at chewing. A dog will not know the difference between a dining chair and a lump of wood in the garden – it's all chew sticks to him.

Insight
A puppy does not discriminate between furniture and a lump of wood.

As an owner you have to redirect his chewing to acceptable items. Provide plenty of safe chewing toys. Kongs are excellent and practically indestructible. Be careful with soft plastic toys that can be chewed to bits in minutes, and can be dangerous if the pieces are swallowed. Roasted bones can be bought from pet shops, but ensure there are no loose splintered bits of bone before giving them to your puppy, and that small pieces do not come off when chewing, as again they can be dangerous if swallowed. If safe, these can be refilled again and again to keep your puppy busy for hours. Kongs and bones can be filled with many different things so your dog need never get bored with them – cream cheese, part of his dinner, marmite, and anything else that he enjoys that is safe to eat.

A stuffed Kong is excellent for discouraging inappropriate chewing if you have to leave your dog alone for a period of time. It will keep him occupied and tire him out while exercising his jaws. If you do catch your puppy chewing an inappropriate item, distract him and ask him to do something you *can* reward with an acceptable chewable alternative.

Jumping up

Jumping up begins when we bring our puppy home; they reach up to get as near to us as possible for greeting, and when they are small and cute we tend to encourage this behaviour by bending down to stroke them. While this is cute, by the time your dog is 8–9 months old and nearly fully grown it is a different story, and a fully grown Labrador jumping up can be dangerous.

Jumping up is one of those behaviours that quickly becomes established. A puppy soon discovers that it is a rewarding pastime and once established it is difficult to break, especially in an older dog. If possible, don't let it start in the first place.

When puppies jump to get attention we inadvertently reinforce it by either pushing them down, telling them 'no' or (for some dogs) looking at them.

Try to get into the habit of greeting your puppy only when he has four paws on the ground or is sitting, especially first thing in the morning, or when you have just come in and your puppy is really excited to see you.

Everyone needs to be consistent with this exercise, including visitors to the house and people he meets out and about. He will then learn that *not* jumping up is the only way to get attention from human beings! Friends or dog-friendly people you meet may tell you that they don't mind the puppy jumping up because they love dogs. This is unfair on your puppy and will confuse him; he won't be able to understand that he can jump up at some people but not at others.

If jumping up has already become a problem with your dog, you need to begin to teach him that he will no longer be rewarded with your attention for jumping up. When he is jumping up, fold your arms and turn your back and avoid eye contact with him. Don't saying anything. Let your body language show him you are not going to interact with him when he is jumping up. As soon as all four paws are on the ground, or he sits, you can immediately praise/reward him for keeping his paws on the ground. Initially you may find he will try even harder to get your attention by jumping up because you have always rewarded it before. Generally these behaviours have to get worse before they improve while your puppy works out what is happening!

Prevention of food guarding

Guarding important resources (important to the dog) is another problem that can be seen in very young puppies, and also one that is frequently unwittingly reinforced. Our dogs will frequently give us signals that are not picked up in the early stages, but that should indicate to us that he is uncomfortable with us being around when he is eating his dinner, chewing a bone or has a 'stolen' item. These signals can be as subtle as becoming very still (freezing) as we approach, flicking his eyes to us and then towards his 'possession', or his mouth may just twitch slightly. If these signals go unheeded and you continue your approach, the dog will find it necessary to escalate the aggression to keep you away. This may start as growling or snarling but can quickly turn into a quick snap and then full-blown biting.

Old-fashioned beliefs were that we needed to ensure that we could remove food from a puppy to ensure it knew we were 'boss'. For many dogs this can be absolutely fine, and they simply look at you a little bemused as you remove his food and then give it back to them. However, if your puppy has previously had to compete with other puppies for food while weaning or even at his mother's teat it is quite possible that he has already learned that he has to fight to keep what is important to him. If we then come along and ignore all the signals and still try to remove his food, and worse still, get cross with him for growling or snarling, we may well quickly confirm to him that he really has to work to keep any resources (food, toys, stolen items). This can rapidly turn into a serious aggression problem that will require the help of a recommended behavioural expert to help you rectify it.

When you first get your puppy home, initially do lots of hand-feeding him some of his dinner so he associates your hands around his food as good news. Sometimes put only half his dinner in the bowl, and as he finishes that, call his name. As he looks up, add some more; repeat this until he has finished his dinner and even add in a few extra tasty treats. This way he will quickly learn that humans being around his food bowl are good news.

Insight

Teach your puppy that people near his food bowl is good news.

This type of exercise should also be practised when he is eating a treat or chew, or playing with a toy. Approach with a higher grade piece of food or toy, when your puppy should leave what he is eating/playing with to take what you are offering. Then you can pick up the object he has just had and return it to him. We are teaching him not to feel threatened by our approach, and that in fact he can usually anticipate that something good is going to happen and he can be quite relaxed in our presence. This should also mean we can remove items from him that he has 'stolen' or got hold of, without a fight or game of chase, by simple swapping it and then removing the item.

Now you can move on to teaching him a 'leave' or 'off' cue (see Chapter 6).

Household etiquette

BY INVITATION ONLY

Always remember to be consistent with your puppy. If you do not want him on the furniture when he is a fully grown dog, then do not let him on the furniture when he is a puppy. It's very easy when he is small and cute to have him on the furniture for a cuddle when he is tired, and children usually like the puppy to be up on the sofa with them to watch the television. Problems arise when your puppy gets bigger and begins to take up more of the sofa, or he comes in from a good run in the park, nice and muddy and now ready for a rest on the sofa, which may well be the last place that you want him to be at that moment.

Make sure that he has a comfortable bed of his own in your lounge. Some breeds of dog are not happy lying on the floor and like something comfortable to rest upon. If you want a cuddle with your puppy, sit on the floor with him.

But if you do want to invite your puppy onto the sofa then that is fine, and it would be a good idea to teach him to get 'on' and 'off' on cue so that you can move him when you want. Do not let your puppy jump off the sofa when he is very small – you don't want to risk damage to his joints or bones. Once he is big enough to get down safely, get a small treat in your hand, lure your puppy off the sofa, and as he is getting off put the cue on the behaviour, (such as 'off'); then repeat the process when getting the puppy 'on'. Practise a number of times through the day, working up to asking the puppy to get 'on' and 'off' without a lure but reward afterwards.

Problems can arise when owners get worked up when the puppy jumps on the sofa, and so when they grab their puppy by the collar to get him off, the puppy gets a fright and may growl at the owner. This is likely to escalate until the problem is out of control, and may well cause future difficulties when your puppy is being handled by the collar, as well as stoking his aggression to stop you removing him from the sofa. In this situation, don't use threats or force to get your dog off the sofa. If he guards the sofa as a comfortable resource then distract him, perhaps by knocking on the front door, blocking his immediate access to that room, and work on teaching him cues to move on and off other things.

RESTRICTED ACCESS

It is wise not to let your puppy follow you around the house all the time; he may become too dependent on you being there and when the time comes when you have to leave him alone he may become very distressed, barking, whining and chewing.

Insight
Do not let your dog follow you round the house all the time.

Use baby-gates strategically around the house so he cannot have continuous access to you. When he is tired, perhaps after a game or a walk, leave him in the kitchen alone in his bed while you get on with other things. He may whine and bark for your attention to begin with, but if you know he does not want to go to the toilet then ignore his whining, otherwise he will learn that he only has to bark and whine for you to come running. If he does whine, go out of the room for a few seconds and wait for quiet. Count to ten and then go back to the puppy while he is still quiet. When he is happy with that interval, on subsequent occasions make the time you are out of the room longer and longer. You can leave your puppy with a Kong stuffed with his dinner so that he has something to occupy him while learning to be alone. You are going to have to leave your puppy alone at some time in his life so the quicker you can teach him that settling down and being alone is not a bad thing, then the easier it will be for him to cope when you do have to start leaving him for short periods.

TABLE MANNERS

If you feed your dog from the table he will quickly learn to nudge you and whine, in anticipation of you giving him a treat. Children are skilled at teaching puppies to beg at tables, especially if they don't like what is on their plate, so they slip it to the dog under the table! To prevent this happening it is useful to use a puppy crate. You can pop him in the crate with a stuffed Kong or hide chew so he is occupied and lying quietly in his crate, and not learning to scrounge at the table. Explain to your children why they should not feed the puppy from their plates. If you don't have a crate, put your puppy's bed in a quiet corner in a different room initially and leave him there with his Kong.

If your puppy is never fed from the table, he will soon realize that there is no point in begging. However, if he realizes that sometimes he does get fed in this way he may pester every time the family sits down to eat.

MANNERS/SELF-CONTROL WITH FOOD

Teaching your puppy to sit and wait for his food will help him learn self-control. If he can control himself enough to wait for his meal, he can begin learning self-control in a wide variety of situations; when other dogs are around, when there are lots of visitors, when he wants his lead put on to go for a walk or even to chase a ball!

Get your puppy's dish (food in it) and ask him to sit. When he is sitting, begin to lower the bowl to the floor. Initially your puppy will begin to get up and move towards the bowl; stand up and wait for him to sit again, repeat the above once more, and don't tell him off for getting up and going towards the bowl; just your action of removing the bowl as he breaks the sit is enough for him to eventually understand that it is his action of getting up out of the sit that causes the food to go away. You will most likely have to repeat this a few more times before you are actually able to place the bowl on the floor while he remains in the sit. The moment his bottom has remained on the floor and you have managed to place the bowl on the floor for just a moment on the first couple of occasions, mark it with a clear signal such as 'good' or 'yes' and tell him to 'get it' or 'it's yours' or something similar, so he understands that not only was sitting the right thing to do but also that he has permission to eat the food. (Useful if you have a dog that tries to steal food or objects if he is used to having to wait for permission to take something!)

Once he is reliably keeping his bottom on the floor you can begin to lengthen the time he remains sitting before you 'mark' him for the correct behaviour and tell him to 'get it'. Always be ready to pick the bowl up if he gets up before you have marked the correct behaviour, then repeat the process, but make sure you don't try to progress too quickly. If he is consistently getting up before you 'mark' him you are probably just asking a little bit too much too early, so go back to the stage at which he was reliable, and build up more slowly. The next stage would be for you to wait for him to give you eye contact before you 'mark' him and then build up on this as above.

Building confidence

If your puppy is a shy puppy (reacts to things going on around him and is slow to recover, or shows lots of apprehension on being introduced to novel things or situations) then you will need to teach him to be confident with the world around him. Socializing him will be slower than training a more confident puppy and you will need to go at a pace that he can cope with, without overwhelming him or forcing him to face his fears. Building confidence can begin in the home; the shy puppy is likely to want to follow you everywhere around the home, including the bathroom and the toilet. Teaching him to be alone for a couple of minutes in another room by leaving him with a few tasty treats or favourite toy will help. (See 'Restricted access' above.)

If your puppy is shy with other dogs and people, it is imperative that you get him in to a reputable puppy class as soon as possible with a trainer who will understand that he needs gentle, careful socializing.

Watch a puppy class first to make sure it is not a free-for-all, where all the puppies are running around causing havoc and learning to bully and be bullied. It is important that you do not force your puppy into situations that he cannot deal with and expect him to get used to it. A seemingly minor incident to you may well be a traumatic event to your puppy, and can have far-reaching consequences that only become evident when he is a bit older. Try to ignore fearful behaviour that your puppy exhibits, so rather than inadvertently reinforcing it by trying to reassure him and telling him it is OK, remove him from the situation and try to relax him at a safe distance with careful use of praise, treats or a game (some expert advice from your trainer or a behaviourist is needed here). Try to be aware of your puppy's fear, and work with him at a distance he is comfortable with initially, and gradually move closer at his pace, until he can cope with it closer up.

For example, a common fear with many puppies is traffic, so taking your puppy down to a busy main street with lots of noisy traffic is not going to help get him confident in traffic if he is really nervous. Instead, take some extra tasty treats and a favourite toy out to a really quiet cul-de-sac and do some training exercises such as watch; sit; down; stand etc. with lots of praise and rewards. When there are no cars moving along the road use lower grade treats, but if a car comes along use a higher grade reward. Work at keeping your puppy's attention while the car is going past, using lots of praise and reward for not reacting to the car because he is so engrossed in interacting with you. It may take many weeks to build up slowly to a busier road, but the end result will be worth the effort, when he is confidently walking along a busy road and not trying to bolt at the sound of a bus coming along or a lorry using its air brakes. (There are many CDs available with instructions on desensitization, with everyday sounds that you come across including traffic, fireworks and similar frighteners; these are useful for desensitizing puppies in a controlled way to the sounds they are likely to encounter.)

10 THINGS TO REMEMBER

1 *It is important that puppies have plenty of opportunity for controlled, appropriate interaction with a variety of other puppies and older dogs, not just the dogs he lives with.*

2 *Avoid rough and tumble games with your dog where he is allowed to bite your clothes (and you).*

3 *How easily your dog is house-trained has a lot to do with you – if you are vigilant, always supervise your dog when he is out of his crate, provide him with plenty of opportunities to relieve himself, stay outside with him and reward him for toileting in the appropriate place it will be achieved quicker.*

4 *Teaching your puppy bite inhibition can be a painful business but is well worth the time spent on teaching him, and is a vital part of his early education.*

5 *Teaching your dog appropriate greeting manners will mean that he will be a welcome visitor and host.*

6 *It is important to build up positive associations around your dog's food bowl.*

7 *Be consistent with your house rules so your dog understands what is required of him.*

8 *Give your dog something to occupy him, like a Kong stuffed with food, when you want to reward him for staying in a room without you.*

9 *Do not fall into the trap of feeding your dog scraps from the table – it will encourage him to beg.*

10 *All puppies learn at different speeds, and more time should be allowed for the shy puppy to become acclimatized to different situations.*

6

Training

In this chapter you will learn:
- *how to teach your dog to respond first time to his name*
- *how to teach your dog to sit on cue*
- *how to teach your dog to come when called.*

Four golden rules

There are four rules to remember when training your puppy or dog.

1 Consistency
This is the most important thing to remember when training your dog. Consistency in all things, but especially in the rules he is expected to understand. If you live on your own with your dog this should be easy to achieve, but if there are several members of a family living together with a dog it is more difficult, but just as important, to be consistent with rules, cues and training methods. For example, if the rule of the house is that the dog should not be fed at the table it is not fair if some people feed him like this; or if he is fed at some extra times (perhaps when Mum is not around) and told off for begging at others. How is the dog supposed to understand the rule if it is being continually broken? Likewise, when first teaching a behaviour, use the same verbal and visual cues – you can change them later if you want to, but when you are first working together it is easier for your dog if you are consistent.

2 Reward behaviour that you want to be repeated

As discussed earlier, rewards vary from dog to dog, but it is important to reward behaviour that you like and want repeated. Sit, down, walk nicely etc. should be rewarded, but so should things as the dog not rushing up to children in the park. Remember: a behaviour that is rewarded (reinforced) is more likely to be repeated. Be aware that you and your dog might have different ideas as to what is rewarding!

3 Ignore behaviour that you don't want

If your dog does something you don't like (but is not dangerous to him or anyone else), ignore it. This is easier said than done, of course, but you need to make a concerted effort to ignore it. For example, if you are on the phone and the dog picks up a tea towel and starts running round with it (to get your attention) DO NOT chase him. A tea towel is not dangerous to your dog, and it can go into the washing machine once he has learned that it is quite boring. If he learns that taking the tea towel is all the invitation you need to join in a great game of 'chase me' he will repeat it again and again. Dogs are excellent trainers!

4 If you can't ignore, then interrupt and ask him to do something you can reward

Sometimes you can't ignore the unwanted behaviour – it might be dangerous, e.g. chewing a phone cable. In this case you need to interrupt him – clap your hands, call his name – and ask him to do something you can reward, e.g. call him to you and ask him to sit. Praise and fuss. By chewing the cable (or taking the tea towel) he is telling you he is bored – find him something else to do. So, after he has returned and sat, have a game/do some training/give him a chew toy (and tuck away the phone cable so he can't get it again!).

Rewards and treats

Rewards and treats come in all different shapes, sizes, tastes and smells to suit every type of taste bud. Ready prepared and packaged treats are easily available and convenient to use. However, some of these products are over-processed and full of colourings and preservatives, and may not agree with your dog.

It is very quick and simple to make your own dog treats. Below are some ideas for treats that can be made in just a few minutes. (See Chapter 13 for further recipes for dogs.)

If you are using food rewards to train your dog, here are a few tips:

▶ *Use small pieces that are easily and quickly chewed and swallowed.*
▶ *When working outdoors it is often more difficult to get your dog's attention. Use food that has a strong smell – garlic sausage or cheese – and is a good motivator for your dog.*
▶ *Liver, chicken and turkey can be cooked quickly and easily.*
▶ *Vary the type of rewards you use to keep your dog's interest.*
▶ *Some dogs enjoy raw vegetables and fruit such as carrots and pieces of apple.*

There are useful toys, such as the Kong, that can be packed with food to keep your dog occupied.

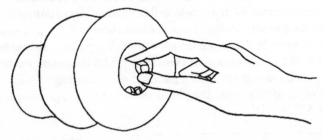

Figure 6.1 A Kong being filled.

Stuffing a Kong:

▶ *First, line the Kong with something soft – fish or meat paste, cream cheese, pâté or something similar.*
▶ *Push something crunchy, such as dog biscuits and carrot into the Kong.*
▶ *Finally, fill the spaces with small tasty pieces of food such as chicken or sausage.*

Who, me?

Your dog's name should get him to look at you expectantly. Building up lots of positive associations with his name will mean he is keen to respond when you use it, rather than completely ignoring you and carrying on with what he was doing. It helps to improve your relationship with him and gain his attention in a variety of situations if you generalize it well.

Try very hard not to use his name as a reprimand or to nag him, nor to call him to you to carry out something that he sees as unpleasant, e.g. cutting his nails, giving him a bath, giving him a worming tablet. Go and get him in those types of scenario. Children can sometimes be guilty of saying their dog's name over and over again, and if you have a few children the sound of his name just becomes background noise to your dog. To get over this, involve your children with the training and explain to them the importance of teaching your dog to respond to his name the first time it is used.

WATCH ME

The basis of all training is being able to get your dog's attention.

Insight
    Before you do any training you need your dog's attention.

When training any new exercise it is best to start with as few distractions around as possible. It makes it far easier for your dog to concentrate and want to pay attention to you!

Wait for your dog to look at your face. Click (mark) and treat.

To give your dog a clue as to what you want, initially you can (for the first couple of times) make a squeaky noise/kissing sound, etc. to attract his attention.

After two or three repetitions he should start looking at you without this instigation. Throw the treat on the floor a short distance away from you at first, so he has to return to you and 'look' at you again.

The next step is to hold a piece of food in one or both hands and put your hands out to the side, level with your shoulder. The dog will naturally want to look at the treat. You should wait for your dog to look at you. (A brief glance is enough at this stage.) If it seems as though he is waiting a long time (or you get bored) you can resort to the kissing sounds.

Begin to throw the rewards a little further from you; he should begin to hurry back to repeat the exercise (he should be learning that paying attention to you is rewarding!).

Once you are confident that you can predict him looking at you, put the behaviour on cue using a word such as 'look', 'watch me' or any word that comes easily to you for this action.

Now you can begin to build up the time he is keeping eye contact with you, varying the time so he has to watch for longer periods. Remember to intermittently reward (sometimes after he has looked at you for three seconds; sometimes ten; sometimes 30; then back to five etc.)

Begin making it a little more difficult for him to get eye contact with you. As he goes off to collect his reward from the floor, start turning away a bit so he has got to come round you to get eye contact. Do this gradually at first, but once he has the idea you should be able to step and turn away and call him to 'watch'.

Repeat the above steps in different locations in the house, and when he is consistently returning and giving you eye contact you can begin to practise in more distracting environments. (Always build up on distractions gradually.)

This exercise is useful when you are out and about and you want your dog to come and pay attention to you while joggers, horses, cyclists and perhaps even a brass band go past. It may be necessary to keep your dog on a lead when you begin to train this exercise outside, but avoid using the lead as an aid to getting his attention; it is simply there to limit his options!

Some dogs may find giving eye contact a little threatening, so you will need to build up the 'watch me' behaviour very slowly and with great care, so your dog can learn that actually eye contact with you is a really good thing.

If your dog already has a history of ignoring you when you call his name, you will have to work extra hard at this exercise. There can be a number of reasons why dogs ignore their handlers, the most common being that the owner (or someone else) has overused their name, calling them when they are not coming back, or when they are being told off for something. This usually happens in the park, when owners only call the dog's name and expect the dog to understand that it means 'I would like you to come here now please!' It is best to call your dog's name (to get his attention) then ask him to 'come' or 'here' (whichever word you have taught him during his recall training). Dogs will also react to the tone of our voice when we are getting frustrated and they will try to keep their head down until we have calmed down. It could also be that they are concentrating hard on what they are doing, chasing or scenting a rabbit or deer for instance; they literally do not hear our call. A dog in a highly aroused state will also be unable to respond to his name, such as a mature male chasing after a bitch in season, or a very territorial dog guarding his garden. An absolutely terrified dog will be completely oblivious to everything.

As with all training, if your dog thinks something is worthwhile he will respond enthusiastically.

Sit on cue

Sit is one of the simplest control exercises and one of the easiest to train. (Although, please be aware that not all dogs find this position comfortable – due to physical conformation or pain.)

Insight

It is generally easy to teach your dog to sit on cue.

It usually comes naturally for a dog to sit in an alert position when expecting something to happen, such as being given food, the owner's return after leaving, or any exciting interaction such as a ball game. The sit/alert position is preferable to the alternatives of pulling on the lead, jumping up or milling around in excitement when anticipating an event. As with all training it is important that your dog fully understands what is expected of him, so you need to be patient and ready to repeat the training over a period of time, in different environments and with varying distractions, until your dog sits instantly on the first cue, and without a food lure.

It is better to have short, interesting training sessions several times a day rather than one long session that may well result in your dog switching off, or you becoming frustrated.

If you teach a person to carry out a task they will usually be able to repeat the job in a different location providing they have the right tools. This ability is known as 'generalizing' a behaviour. Dogs do not generalize as readily as people and different breeds and individual dogs generalize at different rates. This means that if you teach your dog to sit in the living room, you will have to go through the same training in five or six (more in some cases) different places before he generalizes and understands that 'sit' means the same thing in the garden, the park, your friend's house, the vet's surgery, and elsewhere. This is why you will often find at dog training classes that owners say 'he does it at home', when he will not follow cues in a class situation with many distractions around. He is not being naughty; he has not learned the behaviour in enough different locations. Once you have taught him what something means in two or three different locations he generally picks up the idea more quickly as you continue to generalize to other locations.

To help your dog quickly understand that putting his bottom on the floor is the behaviour you want, use a 'marker' (either a clicker or a word such as 'Yes', 'Good' or similar short word) to indicate to your dog he has done the right thing and a reward is to follow.

Insight

Using a marker makes it easier for your dog to understand exactly what he is being rewarded for.

TEACHING A SIT

You will need to gain your dog's attention to begin this exercise (see attention exercise under 'Watch me' above). Once you have gained his attention take a small treat (food lure) and hold it just above the end of his nose. As he starts to sniff it, slowly lift the hand holding the food (still at the end of his nose) and move it over the top of his head but still near his nose. As he is now beginning to lean back in anticipation of the food, his bottom should move towards the floor. As soon as his bottom reaches the floor, 'mark' and give the reward.

If he starts to jump up for the food just ignore this behaviour completely and remove the treat until he settles again. Repeat the exercise (with your hand held a bit closer to his head) until he understands that the only way to get the treat is by placing his bottom on the floor. In many cases the dog will automatically sit quite quickly. Once you have marked the behaviour and given the reward it is fine if your dog gets up. You can 'mark' the sit and throw the food to the floor so your dog has to get out of position to gain the reward, then repeat the above.

Repeat this exercise three or four times using the food lure, then as quickly as possible move on to having no food lure in your hand (have the food in your other hand or a treat pot); but still 'mark' and then treat the sit. (Some dogs are so food-motivated they find it difficult to concentrate with food in the way. Equally you may encourage your dog to become so dependent on food being there he can't possibly do it without food in front of his nose!) This action (moving your hand from in front of his nose and over his head) has now become a hand signal (visual cue) for the dog to sit.

Now you can introduce a verbal cue ('sit') for this action.

Once he is sitting reliably every time you raise your hand he can be introduced to a verbal cue ('sit', or any word you want to use to mean this behaviour).

Begin by saying 'sit' just as you give your hand signal, 'mark' and reward. Repeat this a few times and then begin to say 'sit' just before you give the hand signal. Your dog will start to 'back associate', and learn that every time you say that word 'sit' you give him a hand signal to sit.

Repeat this a number of times and then you can test him to see if he really understands the meaning of the word 'sit'. Say 'sit' and wait just a couple of seconds before you give your hand signal. If he understands the word he should sit before you give the hand signal. Do not keep repeating the word, but if he does not sit immediately, wait a few seconds and give your hand signal until he sits. Some dogs are more auditory than others and the speed with which he responds to your verbal cue will depend on this. Once he responds to one verbal cue without the hand signal, you can go overboard with praise and reward. Now it is time to build up on distractions and generalize the sit to different locations as described for the attention exercise.

Be aware that if you keep repeating your verbal cue ('sit') your dog will learn to sit only after you have repeated the cue three or four times!

When training any new exercise, if your dog does not seem to understand what you want him to do then go back to the stage he was successful at and build up more slowly this time. Your dog will sometimes have an 'off' day or not feel quite as motivated some days, the same as we do. If this seems to be the case, ask your dog for something simple that he knows well, reward and end the training there.

If you find that your dog will only sit using both the verbal and hand signal, then gradually fade out the hand signal reducing the original exaggerated movement over a period until you do not need to use it at all.

Once he fully understands 'sit' you will no longer need to treat him every time he does so; vary the amount he does before he gets a reward, which may mean that sometimes you ask him to sit two or three times before he gets a reward, or you may choose to reward faster sits or sitting for a bit longer (stay).

To extend the time he sits, the aim is for him to maintain the position until you release him, either by marking the behaviour or using a 'release' word such as 'go' or 'OK'.

Initially you will have been rewarding him immediately he sits; now you can begin to delay your marker very slightly and gradually build up on the time he remains in the sit before you mark and release him. If he gets up before you have marked him, do not tell him off. Simply ignore his action – you are probably asking too much too soon. Ask him to sit again, and mark the length of the stay a bit sooner.

Once you start to generalize the sit and are training it in more distracting situations, it is wise to upgrade the type of reward you use to take this into account, and keep your dog focused on you when there are other things going on around him. Tasty frankfurters or a piece of cheese often works well and are far more interesting than a piece of kibble from his dinner.

Ideally you should be in control of the distractions from the outset. This means that you set them up with friends and family. For example, your dog should still sit if another family member comes into the room. You can then ask him to sit when members of the family come into the room and move around or talk to each other. You can build on this using willing family and friends and other well-behaved dogs. Be creative, think of different distractions and locations where you would like your dog to sit instantly on cue, and train with this in mind.

Down

This is one of the most useful control exercises to teach your dog, second only to the recall. Teaching your dog to lie down instantly on command is not only impressive for onlookers, but can make life a lot easier and safer for both dog and owner.

Insight
An instant down is a very useful control exercise.

If you meet a small child or a nervous adult when you are out walking your dog, the down position is much less threatening than a dog running around barking. If you need to attend to an emergency; for instance, someone has fallen over and you need to help, you can ask your dog to lie down, while you attend to the problem. Supposing you see some imminent danger when your dog is off the lead – how reassuring to know that you can stop him in his tracks with a distant down command.

For some breeds, such as Border Collies, the down is often a default position. Others, like Lurchers who have very deep chests, find that the down is not necessarily a comfortable position and may be harder to train. There are two down positions – the *alert*, ready to move 'down', in which the dog holds his body straight, rests on his elbows and holds his head up; and there is the *relaxed* 'down', in which he relaxes onto one side or the other, which naturally bends his body slightly and lowers the head. The alert down is usually the first position, but most dogs will go into the relaxed down if they remain down for any length of time. The relaxed down is preferable for a stay, and some people actually teach their dog to lie on his side for this.

From an early age you can start teaching your dog what the word 'down' means. To do this, simply say the word 'down' whenever you see him in the down position. Make sure that a pleasant experience always follows, either a gentle stroke or some calm praise: 'Down – what a good dog!' You could even drop a treat between his front feet. This is called 'capturing' the behaviour.

If yours is one of the unusual dogs who is not interested in food and you have tried all sorts of different treats such as cheese and sausage, then you will have to look more deeply into what he might find rewarding. Perhaps he likes to play tuggie, chase a ball, or just have his chest rubbed. (It needs to be something your dog enjoys and wants to work at getting you to give him, not necessarily something *you* enjoy!)

Whatever reward you are going to use, pair it with your 'marker' as described earlier.

TEACHING THE DOWN

Once again, choose a training area where there are no distractions. Hopefully by now your dog will be eager to pay attention to you.

Begin by getting your dog's attention. Ask your dog to sit (initially for many dogs it is easier to learn the down from the sit position).

Take your chosen food reward and show it to him while he is in the sit. Enclose the food with your hand so that your fingers are downwards. It is often easier to be crouched down with the dog at this stage. Hold the hand with the food in it under the dog's nose keeping it about half an inch away. Slowly move your hand towards the floor, aiming just between his front paws, keeping the food close to his nose and enclosed by your fingers.

If you are lucky enough that your dog goes down immediately, mark and reward the behaviour as soon as his elbows touch the floor. Do not use the cue 'down' yet. He has no idea what it means at this stage, and we will introduce it in the same way as for the 'sit' exercise. It is quite likely that your dog will not go down the full way on the first few occasions, so at the moment be prepared to take an approximation of the down; it may be just his head moving towards the floor to start with, then he bends one elbow, then both elbows, and then his chest will touch the floor. Mark and give him a treat at each stage, and maybe give him several pieces and a game when he achieves the full 'down' so he is aware that chest and elbows on the floor is the position that gets the most rewards. Each stage of the above should be marked and rewarded, but we are just going to hold out a bit longer the next time for a further approximation. This is called 'shaping a behaviour' in which we can picture the finished behaviour and mark and reward any movements in the right direction towards this end goal.

When he has begun to go all the way into the down position, you must always hold out for the full down, so this is where you may need to be a bit patient as he works it all out. Hold out for the full down, then instantly mark and reward and give lots of praise. Don't worry if he gets up straight away – you will be able to extend the length of time he stays down in due course exactly the same as you do in the sit exercise.

Once your dog is consistently going down on your visual cue (the hand action) you can begin to introduce the verbal cue (same as for the sit). Give the verbal cue at the same time as you give the visual cue initially, then after a few repetitions you can say 'down' just a couple of seconds earlier than the visual cue so your dog can back associate the use of the word 'down'; this is followed by the hand signal that he goes down on. Once he is happy going down on both cues you may want to start fading the visual cue a little bit at a time, so maybe stand up and point to the ground, gradually standing straighter and straighter so that your dog can hopefully begin to go down on mainly a verbal cue without a visual at all (very useful as an emergency stop).

If your dog does not seem to be able to go into the down position using the above method (sometimes they keep bobbing up from the sit, especially the smaller breeds of dog) you can try to teach the down with the dog initially in a standing position. Use a treat in your hand as above. Hold the treat near to the dog's nose and slowly lower it to the ground, moving in towards the dog's chest and between his paws. It is quite likely he will adopt a 'bow' position, which you can mark and reward and gradually shape until his bottom touches the floor; then mark and give a big reward and lots of praise.

Alternatively, you can sit on the floor with one leg bent at an angle with just enough room for your dog to tunnel under. Use a tasty treat and hold it at the opposite side of your leg to that of the dog and lure him through the 'tunnel'. Once again it is likely that you will have to do this in stages and mark and reward each approximation of the 'down'. Reward him for putting his head under your leg, then head and shoulders, then laying down under your leg. Do not use your leg to push down on him as he is coming through, as this may scare him and stop him doing it altogether. Also, if he is very keen to come under your leg make sure you don't just lure him so that he comes through and finishes in a standing position. Once he is comfortably dropping into the down under your leg you can begin to raise your leg, and fade, or reduce its importance as a prompt. Begin to introduce your cue word once you have faded the leg.

Whichever method you have chosen to use, you now need to go through the same stages of generalizing the behaviour to different locations (see attention exercise) and begin to build up on duration and distractions.

When your dog fully understands the cue when there are no distractions, you need to retrain the exercise in at least six different places, gradually introducing more and more distractions. Maybe you start the training in your living room when the rest of the family are all out for the evening. Next it could be when the family are home, then in the garden, then the park or perhaps a friend's garden. Distractions can be people, noises, other dogs, aeroplanes overhead, motorbikes roaring past and all sorts of other everyday happenings.

Do not be discouraged if your dog does not immediately understand the cue in a new place. You may well have to virtually go back to stage one with him in each venue, but it will be quicker each time. You will know that he fully understands the cue the first time you take him somewhere new to train and he drops into the down position immediately when asked.

Most of all, make training fun for you and your dog.

Stand

The 'stand' is an exercise that is often overlooked or only seen as useful to teach if you are thinking of showing your dog, or taking part in obedience type training and are thinking of entering competitions. But the stand is an extremely useful exercise.

Insight
Stand is often undervalued as an exercise to teach.

For example, if your dog can stand in position while the vet carries out a health check, including taking his temperature, feeling his abdomen, and generally checking him over, the whole experience can be less stressful for everyone. (Especially if you have done lots of handling exercises with him.) It is also useful when you need to dry your dog, groom him, take burrs and grass seeds out of his coat or inspect him for lumps or bumps.

Teaching the stand is very easy. Hold a small treat between your finger and thumb and ask your dog to sit. Show your dog the treat just in front of his nose, bring it slowly forward in a straight line (keeping it at the height of your dog's shoulder and parallel to the ground). As your dog moves forward to follow the lure drop your hand very slightly – this encourages his bottom to remain in the stand position as his head is looking down – mark and reward. You only want your dog to stand, not walk, so move slowly. The way that you move your hand with the treat then becomes your hand signal for the stand. When your dog is moving into the stand without hesitation, this is the time to put the behaviour on cue. Say 'stand' just as you move your hand forward so he starts to associate the word with the action. Mark and reward. Then once again it's time to generalize and build up on distractions.

Walking on a loose lead

Lead walking is often a confusing exercise as there are so many ways of stopping a dog from pulling, including some very useful training aids, some of which we will explore. Firstly, you need to decide what you want when you and your dog go for a walk. Is it a dog that sticks to the leg like Velcro as though doing obedience at Crufts? Or a walk that you and your dog can enjoy together without having your arm wrenched out of its socket and your dog choking on the collar? Most owners want the latter and that is what this section aims to achieve.

Before we work on the actual exercise, we need to have a little understanding about why dogs pull. Is it because they are excited about where they are going? Is it because they want to be in front all the time? Are they being dominant (a traditional line of thought)? It is simply that the owner has *taught* their dog that pulling is OK – albeit inadvertently. Look at what happens the first time a lead and collar are put on a puppy. The owner invariably winds the lead around their hand and makes the lead taut, then when the puppy pulls towards something they follow, the puppy stops and has a sniff and then pulls towards something else. The owner either follows *or* pulls the puppy in another direction. The puppy has learned that strength matters; if you want to get to something or go somewhere you need to pull and if that doesn't work then you need to pull harder!

Consider how dogs and puppies learn. They learn through experience and reward. If the experience is rewarding then they are more likely to repeat it. If pulling on the lead results in your dog/puppy getting to what it wants, that is reward enough. Randomly reward any behaviour and it strengthens. So sometimes allowing your dog to pull and other times not allowing him to pull will only strengthen the pulling behaviour! Some dogs really enjoy pulling just for the sake of it. By the time your dog is an adult he is a seasoned puller, and can often make walking the dog an unpleasant experience (for you).

Traditional methods, such as those used by the late Barbara Woodhouse, relied on aversive methods to train 'heel work'. A choke chain was worn by the dog, which meant that it could only be walked on one side, usually the left, and when the dog walked out in front, the owner was instructed to shout 'heel' and then jerk the dog back to their side. This type of training relies on the dog learning to avoid the aversive pain of the choke chain tightening. The dog hears the 'heel' cue, waits for the jerk and then returns to the owner's side. Eventually some dogs learn to remain by the owner's side in order to avoid the uncomfortable jerk, while others spend a lifetime being pulled and jerked around. Those dogs that continue to pull despite the choke chain can be distinguished by the bald patch of brittle hair from the continual friction of the chain. There is no place for the choke chain in modern dog training.

Developments in dog training have led to a better understanding of how dogs learn and how best to train them. There are various methods used by trainers to teach lead walking, and numerous pieces of equipment that promise to stop dogs pulling, some of which will be discussed.

Let's look at some of the techniques used by modern trainers.

LURE AND REWARD

The dog can walk on your left or on your right. For ease of explanation I will assume that your dog is going to walk on your left. If if you want him to walk on your right, just reverse the instructions. It is a good idea to get your dog used to walking nicely on both sides, but don't let him cross sides when he feels like it because this can easily trip you up if you are caught unawares.

> Very important: if at any time during the exercise your dog pulls, stand still and keep the hand holding the lead in the same position. Your dog is pulling for a reason – perhaps to get somewhere faster, to investigate a smell, or to reach another dog. If you let him pull you towards his target then you are rewarding him for pulling.

Walking on a loose lead is hard work for your dog, so make sure the treats are high grade, at least when you start. If your dog is not food-motivated then by all means use a toy, but it does make things slower if each time you reward you have to stop and have a game. So, if he finds food rewarding (and most do if you choose the right food) try to use that.

Hold the dog's lead in your right hand, and have some treats ready in your left hand.

Get your dog's attention and, using the treat lure him into position (ask him to follow the treat) until he is standing beside you, facing the same way as you are. Then give him the reward.

Using the food in your left hand, lure him forward a step or two and as long as the lead is loose, reward him. Take a few more steps, reward again, and repeat for as long as he is walking with a loose lead. You may find he dashes off after getting the reward – do not move! Stand steady, and when he stops pulling get his attention and lure him back into position beside you, take a couple of steps, reward.

If you are clicker training you will know that it is important to 'mark' the exact behaviour, i.e. walking without pulling, before rewarding. You may find it easier to use your click word (marker word) rather than the clicker itself – you have lots of things in your hand anyway. If you are not clicker training I would still suggest that you mark the behaviour. To do this, as your puppy is walking on a loose lead say 'good' or 'yes', and then feed him a treat when he is standing still. In this way he will know that he is getting a reward for walking nicely, but by feeding him when he is standing still you are lessening the risk of him choking on the food. If you just fed him when he was standing still (without marking the loose lead walking behaviour) then he will think that you want him to keep stopping – not good.

When your dog is able to walk two or three steps on a loose lead you can start to increase the distance between treats. Reward him for three of four steps walking nicely, then maybe four or six, then for three again gradually stretching out the distance between treats, but remember; do not just increase the gaps, surprise him by sometimes rewarding for just a couple of steps.

Once your dog is able to walk about ten paces without pulling you might want to put in a cue word – 'walk nice', 'with me' or similar work quite well. While training this exercise it is important that you say what the dog is *doing* rather than what you want him to do, i.e. if he is walking nicely, say so. If he is pulling and you say 'walk nice' (before he understands the cue) he will think that 'walk nice' means pull like a train! On the same note, if you do not have time to stand still if he pulls, or reward lots of nice walking – perhaps you are rushing to meet the children or similar – then when he does pull it is better to say 'pull'. In this way he will associate the word with his action. Or you could get a training harness and put this on him when you are not able to do the training (see Chapter 2). A training h̶a̶ forward movement when he pulls.

Remember that this is a training exercise, a tiring for your dog at the outset. It might be the exercise to your dog in the living room, or actually taking him out to practise. Keep the tr̶ few minutes at a time at the start. If you begin b̶y full walk using this exercise you will have a very t̶ ̶.̶.̶.̶ ̶.̶.̶e end of it, and then the training will not be so much ̶.̶.̶ him.

The second method you might like to try is:

RED LIGHT/GREEN LIGHT

This exercise is based on the understanding that each step you take energizes the dog.

Stand still and wait for your dog to stop pulling, so the lead goes loose – reward. Give him the reward when he is beside you. In this way he will learn that being beside you is a good place to be.

Take one step – your dog may well rush off. Stand still and again wait for him to come back and stand beside you. This may take several minutes, so be patient. Reward.

Take one more step – this time your dog should come back to your side a bit quicker. Reward again.

When you can take one step without the dog rushing off, you can try two steps. Do not be surprised if he dashes off again. Stand still and wait for him to come back. Reward by your side.

Two steps, wait, dog returns, reward.

When he can walk two steps without dashing off, increase to three. When he can cope with three steps, increase to four and so on.

...e first step it can take quite a long time for your ...loosen the lead/come back to you, but if you are ...e will stand still eventually. Do not be tempted to pull him ...k, just wait. The time it takes for him to loosen the lead will lessen each time. But when you add in another step the time may increase again. You might need to take just one step at a time for several steps, but again as the exercise progresses so the intervals between increasing the steps will get shorter and shorter.

As with the previous exercise, do not introduce your cue word until he is managing several paces, and do not continue the exercise for more than a few minutes.

Taking your dog for a walk should be enjoyable for both of you. Remember that he is going out not just for the exercise but for stimulation – let him have time to sniff where other dogs have been. Just don't let him pull you to the places and do expect him to come away from the smell when you ask him to!

There are a few different ways to teach loose lead walking, but the end result is the same; your dog is walking with you without pulling in front or dragging behind.

The secret to training loose lead walking is rewarding the behaviour you want, and not rewarding unwanted behaviour.

If your dog pulls ahead, stand still. Don't drag him back or allow him to progress. Put your hands against your tummy and stand still. Standing like this will restrict your dog's movement considerably. Eventually he will realize that he is going nowhere and will either wander back to you or at least look at you to see why you are not moving.

If he looks at you, encourage him to come back to your side, facing the same direction that you are walking. Take a couple of steps forward, click or treat.

You should click while your dog is moving, but if appropriate you can stop before giving a food reward.

Stay

There is sometimes controversy over the use of the 'stay' cue, as opposed to a 'wait'. For the purpose of this exercise we will assume that stay means 'stay exactly where you are without moving until I come back to you.' You can use 'wait', to indicate to your dog 'wait where you are until I tell you to do something else'; and also 'settle', which can be used to indicate to your dog that nothing much is happening so go and find somewhere comfortable to settle down.

If you wish to take part in The Kennel Club Good Citizen Dog Scheme Club Tests, Obedience, Agility, Working Trials, Gundog Tests and many other dog activities your dog will need to understand the 'stay' cue. On a practical day-to-day level it is extremely useful if you can depend on your dog to stay in one place. 'Stay' is useful in an emergency; for example, if you need to deal with an accident or if a bottle of milk has broken on the kitchen floor. It can also be used when you meet a friend on a walk and stop for a chat, and it really helps to have a good stand/stay for grooming. A dog that you can trust to stay in one place while you are busy dealing with something else is a pleasure to live with.

To build up a solid, reliable 'stay' your dog needs to understand that he maintains the required position until he is released by you, despite any distraction, at any distance from you and for varying lengths of time. Each of these requirements – distance, duration and distractions – need to be built up gradually, and individually, over a period of time to really establish a solid, reliable stay.

The following method describes how to teach the sit/stay. The same applies for the 'down' and 'stand' stays. I personally don't use a 'stay' cue, but being humans we tend to want to talk to our dogs, and many people like to add in a 'stay' when they require their dog to maintain a position. If you have taught your stationary positions (sit, down, stand) reliably, by generalizing them as described earlier in the sit exercise, you will have effectively begun to teach your dog to stay. Now it is just a case of building up on reliability.

Once your dog can sit every time he is asked to do so, in any location, begin to teach the 'stay' by standing next to your dog while he is sitting. You are now going to let your dog know it is very rewarding to remain sitting. After he has sat for a couple of seconds, give him a treat, without marking the behaviour (because that would indicate the exercise was over). We are now letting your dog know that remaining in this position is what makes you treat him. Gradually start to randomly reward your dog for sitting beside you for two seconds, five seconds, ten seconds, back to three seconds and so forth. Your dog should remain sitting and looking at you expectantly for the next reward to arrive. It is fine to tell him he is a good boy for sitting or staying if you prefer, and the treats will help to confirm that he is doing the right thing.

Don't be tempted to rush at this stage. If he gets up before you have reinforced his position with a treat, it is likely that you are trying to move too fast. Go back to the last stage he was successful at and build up again. When you begin this exercise, don't ask him to remain sitting for more than 30 seconds and that is with lots of food reinforcements on a variable schedule (see above). Get to about 30 seconds and break off the exercise frequently (using your marker to indicate that the exercise is over) and reward with a game before you begin again. When you are confident that he understands that sit means he remains sitting while you are standing next to him, you can begin to build up on distance.

Start by taking one pace away from your dog either to the front or to the side while he is sitting. Quickly step back and reward, then take a step away and count to two before returning; next, step in a different direction and return and treat. Continue to verbally praise him while he is still sitting and staying. To start with, only leave your dog for one or two seconds before returning to him. At this stage, each time you return to your dog give him a food treat as a reward. When you end the exercise, use your marker and have a game to make it a very obvious difference between the treats for remaining in one position and a big reward for exercise over!

Initially your dog may well move when you take a step away (it is natural that he will want to follow you). Try not to go so far away that he is tempted to break his stay (get up from the sit). Small, successful, stages are always more effective. If he does break, ask him to sit again and build up in slower stages. The secret is to move away and back within a second at first, so that your dog does not even have time to move. Once he understands that your moving away means you will be returning with treats, he will get the idea and you can begin to build up on varying the time and distance you are away from him, and eventually – if you want to – build up to out-of-sight stays. All the above steps need to be taught separately and then combined together to create a reliable stay in any location.

Before building up on distractions it is a good idea to generalize the stay to several different locations. Then you can begin to build up on distractions while he remains in the sit. When you start to build in distractions you will need to go back to rewarding more frequently while you remain close to him, then once more introduce the distance as above, taking it at your dog's pace and remembering not to ask too much of him too soon. Each time you increase the distractions you need to start at the beginning and build up again. This may sound rather laborious, but if you want to have a really solid, reliable stay with your dog, you need to ensure he fully understands what you expect of him.

Insight

Build up distance, duration and distractions separately.

Wait

Quite often without realizing it, many owners have already done the groundwork for teaching their dog to wait. This happens when they are being taught manners before their dinner for example (for 'table manners' see Chapter 5 'Household etiquette' section). Teaching a dog to wait until further instructions, or permission to carry on with what he is doing, can be very useful in many areas of your day-to-day living with your dog.

Once he understands the concept of waiting before he is given permission to eat his dinner, you can begin to repeat the exercise with a piece of food. In exactly the same way as with his dinner, ask him to sit, lower the treat (low grade at this stage – biscuit, piece of dried dog food or similar) towards the floor. As he gets up in anticipation of getting the food, stand up (taking the treat with you) and ask him to sit again. Repeat the exercise until he can remain in the sit while you lower the food all the way to the floor. It is a good idea to pick the food up and give him it or pick it up and throw it to one side as you say 'get it' or 'OK' (permission to eat the treat) because it means you can actually combine teaching a 'wait' or a 'leave it' (see section later in this chapter on 'leave') and he will also be practising his self-control. Once he is reliable doing this you can increase the grade of food used and also start to use his toys as well.

Repeat this training in as many different places as you can, e.g. the kitchen, lounge, garden, out on a walk.

You can introduce this cue into situations where it will be useful in your everyday dealings with your dog. Another way of using the wait is to use it to allow you to go through the door first. It can save you being barged aside by a large dog who is keen to get out for his walk, or who wants to get onto the sofa first!

Begin, as with all new exercises, in a situation where you are most likely to succeed. This would not be at walk time while standing by the front door with a lead in your hand, but more likely after a long walk and returning to the house, or perhaps going from the kitchen to the dining room. Ask your dog to sit and once he is sitting, reach out and slowly begin to open the door. He is likely to make a move towards the door. Close it again and ask him to sit, say 'wait' and repeat the above until you are able to fully open the door while he remains sitting; then you can either step through and say 'OK' or go through, and this means he can proceed. (Take care that you do not hit your dog with the door when closing it.

You do not want your dog to be frightened of doors.) What will be learning here is that his behaviour of getting up causes the door to close, so it is best for him to remain in the sit position until the door is opened and he will be given permission to go through. Practise this on as many internal doors as possible before progressing to the door that leads to the outside and the greatest reward of all – a walk! When you come to do this exercise at the front door, attach his lead as if you are going for a walk and follow the same procedure. Ask him to sit and wait until the door is opened, then you can say it's OK to go. It is best not to do this exercise for the first time if you are in a hurry to get out for a walk as it may take a while the first time you do it!

The 'wait' exercise can be used to teach your dog to wait when getting in and out of the car. This can be of vital importance especially when getting him out of the car, as you need to have your dog under control when he is excited about his walk and where there may be other cars, dogs and people. The easiest option is getting him into the car; remember to always start with the easiest option first. You want your dog to succeed, not fail. With the lead on, walk up to the car and give the wait cue. Open the door and reward him for not jumping in. If he goes to jump in, close the door (again being careful that he doesn't get hit by it). As before, once he is waiting you can tell him to get in the car. The same principle is applied to jumping out of the car, but be aware that he is likely to be more excited if the car means the park, so open the door a fraction as you did initially in the house door exercise. If he makes a move to get out, close the door and wait a moment. Then repeat as before until you can fully open the door while he is still waiting and you can tell him it's OK to get out. It might help if you have someone sitting in the car with your dog, so if he does decide to make a dash for it the person can hold his lead.

Recall

The recall is the most important exercise that you can teach your dog or puppy. Most owners want to enjoy taking their dog for a

s safe to do so, let them off lead so they can
d play as dogs should. If you can't let your
cause you worry that he might not come back,
to a life on the lead whenever he goes out. This
ial skills with other dogs, because he needs
and greet. Being kept on the lead will also increase
frustration and reduce opportunities to explore his environment,
which is necessary for mental stimulation.

Insight

Recall is probably the most important exercise you can teach
your dog.

Why do many people find this exercise so difficult? Let's look firstly
at what a recall should mean. As an owner you should be able to call
your dog and your dog should respond by returning to you. Simple!
Why do so many dogs not comply? There are two main reasons;
firstly, he has never been taught to recall, owners just expect that
if they call their dog's name, their dog will return to them. Maybe
he will – if there are no other distractions! Secondly, your dog will
often associate the call with the end of fun and freedom and decide
that he would rather stay in the park playing with other dogs or
investigating his environment. This 'disobedience' can lead to
frustration on the part of you, the owner, who is likely to tell the dog
off, thus making him even less likely to want to return next time.
Why would a dog want to return to an owner who is unpleasant?
Understanding this will help you with the recall programme.

So, firstly, you need to *teach* a recall in exactly the same way as
you have built up on all the other exercises – starting with no
distractions, and generalizing to different locations before you
begin to add in more distractions. As distractions are added in,
then the quality/grade of the reward needs to be increased, varied
and fun-related, so your dog is always keen to return to you no
matter what is going on!

It is important to remember that the 'reward' needs to be what
your dog sees as rewarding, not what *you* think it might be. There

is little contest between dried kibble and tasty meat off-cuts or baked liver! The harder the work, e.g. doing a recall when near other dogs, the bigger and better the reward needs to be during training. You may consider that your affection, patting and soft vocal tones are rewarding, but your dog may get these throughout the day for the merest compliance or for just 'being', so it doesn't have the same value as a tasty treat that is produced at varying times.

The way you deliver your rewards can also add variety; for example, scattering a few treats on the floor in front of your feet as your dog gets to you means you have plenty of time to take hold of his collar if need be. Another way is to throw pieces of bouncy sausage backward and forward along the floor, low so your dog sees them, and throwing them further as he gets the idea of chasing them. As he picks up one piece, call him back to you, throw out another piece and repeat three or four times. Most dogs really enjoy this game. You may find that for some dogs, food takes second place to a game with a ball or tuggie. If your dog has a favourite toy and you keep it special by only allowing limited access to it, this will also act as a high-grade reward. If at present your dog is not particularly interested in a toy, start playing several times a day for short exciting games, but finish while he is still having lots of fun and put it aside until the next time you play. Knowing what your dog finds rewarding is the first step to a successful recall. You can use two balls in a similar way to the sausage game; throw a ball out, and as he brings it back show him the other ball and throw it out, so that he spits the first ball out and runs after the new one, and repeat. If your dog has a good retrieve to hand then you can just use one ball.

TRAINING PUPPIES

If you are training a puppy then your job is much easier than training an older dog who has already learned not to come back. Puppies have a natural inbuilt insecurity, and when very young are generally keen to stick close to you as they come to terms with all the strange things they are beginning to meet in the big wide world. So letting them off lead early will help progress your recall. But actually taking them to a park and unclipping the lead off your puppy is a pretty scary thing to do for the first time. If you are anxious about this, it can be helpful to find a smaller enclosed area, a field or tennis court where you can shut yourself in and let your puppy off in safety; or attach a 20–30 foot piece of guy line from a camping shop to his fixed harness, tie a few knots in it along the way, and if you need to you can quickly retrieve your puppy this way. Avoid chasing any loose puppy, they will generally run away from you. If in doubt then use a long line until your recall is well practised. When you are practising, use trees to hide behind (as long as you can keep an eye on your puppy) and put a little doubt in your puppy's mind about where you are. This will encourage him to keep an eye on you, as in his eyes you are a bit unpredictable and could disappear at any minute.

UNDERSTANDING

Owners often think that dogs are being deliberately disobedient; they run off, and when you call them they ignore you. But look at it from a different angle. Imagine that you are watching the television and it's your favourite programme or an interesting news report, then suddenly a family member says loudly, 'Are you listening to me? I'm talking to you'. The answer is no you weren't listening; you could not fully concentrate on more than one thing at a time!

Insight
It is difficult for your puppy to concentrate on you while he is taking in lots of information.

Now understand that your dog, when he's out in the field taking in all that information through his senses, all those smells, all those sounds, has his concentration fully taken up with processing that information and it is hard for him to hear your calls.

If, while you were watching that television programme the phone rang, that would break through your level of concentration and you would respond. Similarly, having taught a good recall or introduced a whistle in the correct way, your dog will find it difficult not to respond.

The following recall programme is designed in three stages; each needs to be worked on before moving to the next. The aim is to have a dog which will return to you on the first calling, not one that comes when you have called three, four, five or six times. Read the whole programme before you start and keep a note on how well each stage is going so that you can see the progress your dog is making.

First stage

This stage is for any dog, any age, irrespective of previous learning. Whether you have a puppy who has not started training or an older dog who comes back 'sometimes', you start here!

You will need treats (really tasty and no bigger than about a quarter of a choc drop), a favourite toy – one your dog gets really excited about – and a whistle; this doesn't have to be a 'dog' whistle, but can be a gun dog whistle or a referee's whistle. The benefit of these types of whistle is that you will know how loud they sound. A long line, possibly a lunge line used for horse training is useful, available from horse equipment suppliers (not an extending lead, these are not suitable for this exercise) and patience! You will also need to give thought as to what you are going to 'call' to your dog, e.g. your dog's name and your recall word – 'come' or 'here' or 'come here' are good. This recall phrase will need to be consistent; you cannot begin the training with, for example, 'Bonny come' and later shout 'come here Bonny'!

Work in a familiar room that is quiet. Hold the treats so that your dog or puppy can see them and give one or two just to get him interested and to keep his attention. At this point you do not need to say anything. Next, remain where you are and say the recall cue and then give another treat, repeat this several times being sure to say the recall cue *before* you give the treat, not at the same time. You are building an association between the words and the treats.

Next, take one step backwards and call once; do not be tempted to call and call, be patient and wait for the response. Some dogs will move immediately, others will stand and work out what it is that you want, but if you have built the association between the recall cue and the treat your dog will respond. That was your first 'one call' recall! Repeat the whole process at least three times.

Next, do exactly the same exercise, but this time before you give the treat, take the collar. This adds extra control in the early stages, especially for those dogs who previously have come to within a hand's distance from you and run off again!

It is important to reward your dog as soon as he gets to you. Don't ask your dog to sit. If you do, you will be rewarding the sitting and not the recall, and later you can add the sit if you want to. Remember, your dog needs to build the association between the recall and the reward. Begin to put a greater distance between you and your dog. Get other family members to join in and play a 'round robin' game in which he is called from one family member to another, each person giving him a reward when he recalls to them, remembering to call just once and wait for a response. Your dog may find it hard at first to move away from the one who has just rewarded him until he realizes that everyone has treats if he just goes where he's called.

Start to move outside (to a secure garden) and call him from outside to inside and vice versa, stopping before your dog loses enthusiasm. This new 'game' (if you always keep it fun it will be a game as far as your dog is concerned) can be played any time during the day; you will be working on making this a 'hard-wired' response.

INTRODUCING THE WHISTLE
If you want to introduce a whistle, this is the best time. It is especially useful for dogs which do not respond to your present recall cue.

The whistle can make your recall more reliable, for when your dog's attention is fully on other things the sound of the whistle will interrupt his concentration and bring him back to you; plus it is always a consistent sound, unlike your voice.

Insight

A whistle is useful when teaching the recall.

Decide how you wish to make the whistle sound. Just like your recall cue, it must be the same every time. Try it when your dog is out of earshot. Try one 'peep', try 'peep peep', and see which you prefer. Just before you make your next recall blow the whistle and then call your dog. Your dog should recognize the whistle after about four or five recalls. This is now part of your recall and should be used every time you are out. You do not need to use it in the house but a little practice now and again will be beneficial. From now on, when we say 'recall' this implies that you should use your whistle (if you have chosen to) and call. You will notice that your dog is responding as soon as you blow the whistle and already returning to you before you get the 'call' in, but don't drop the recall cue. You need to use the two together for some time to come.

During the first stage you will need to be certain that each call is successful and productive. It will also mean that if you feel that your dog is unlikely to come when called, perhaps when he is engrossed in something, then you should not call him but go and get him. There is no need to say anything to him, pop his lead on and carry on with your walk.

You will be able to practise the recall away from home if the chosen area is safe and free of major distractions such as other dogs. This is the time to use the long line attached to a fixed harness if you are not confident that you can recall your dog quickly should the need arise. If you have a friend with you, take it in turns to call your dog backwards and forwards between you. When you get more confident that your dog will return, you can let go of the line and allow it to drag on the ground. Your dog will have more choice as to whether he comes back to you, but you will have the reassurance that you can grab the long line if necessary. Be careful that the line can't snag on anything, and wear gloves to avoid friction burns if you do need to grab the line.

This is the stage where you may find the food that you have been using is less interesting, and you may need to increase its palatability, possibly introducing new foods that your dog has not had before. This should keep his interest going for a while. If you have been playing toy games with your dog, this is when it will pay dividends. This is the chance to use the toy as a reward. When you next call your dog and he begins to return to you, get his toy out, perhaps a ball on a rope and throw the ball behind you in an excited manner so that your dog sees it and increases his speed in order to chase the ball. This works very well with dogs that like to chase, such as collies, GSDs, terriers and sight hounds.

Practise the first stage until you have a good, fast response. Begin to reward the quicker responses, but use just verbal praise for the mediocre ones. Never tell your dog off for not responding to you; just don't reward him until he responds, and then with verbal praise. But next time he responds instantly let him know he has done well, that you are really pleased with him and give him a high-grade food reward or a game.

Stage two
Having been taught a good response without distractions, your dog needs to progress to the skill of responding with distractions.

Once again you will start in the house. You will know your dog well enough by now to know what he finds distracting. Make it easy to begin with, such as a family member holding food, but not letting your dog have it. When your dog shows interest in the food being held, recall your dog once, and wait. Watch for any signs of response, call again if necessary, and wait. It is important to allow your dog time to respond. Later your dog will respond quicker. As soon as your dog begins to respond, move backwards away from the distraction so that your dog has to follow you. Now play with your dog or give a really tasty treat. Your dog has just worked really hard! Now your dog gets a second reward, he gets to go back to the distraction if he wishes. Repeat the process a few times and then take the distraction you are using away. Your dog will now have started to learn that coming away from distractions is rewarding.

Practise in the garden with distractions of increasing difficulty, such as children playing ball games or someone holding his favourite toy. You are now ready to take your dog to the park and practise, taking your long line with you. You can either keep your dog on the line, or take it off and call him back before another dog arrives. When you see another dog in the distance and before your dog spots it, call your dog to you and attach the long line to his harness, if you haven't already done so. When the other dog comes close enough, allow the dogs to meet and greet, making sure that the line does not hamper them or become tight in any way. Once they have met, recall your dog and wait for a response. You may need to call a second time, and as soon as your dog responds, produce your toy to play with unless, of course, the food that you have is more rewarding. Treat your dog and tell him he can now go back to the other dog! Repeat the process, this time keeping your dog on the lead and continuing your walk, allowing your dog off the lead once the other dog is out of sight.

At this stage, should your dog see another dog and you do not have him on the lead or long line, do not expect him to come back if you call him. He needs lots more practice. If he is not going to return to you, you will just have to let him meet the other dog! If necessary, go up to your dog and put the lead on. Do not keep repeating your cue to return to you. Move away from the distraction and do some attention exercises that you can reward, allowing your dog back to the other dog if appropriate. Practise this stage for a few weeks; the responses should get better, especially if you are playing with your dog when he comes to you. When you feel that 99 per cent of the time your dog will recall away from another dog while on the long line you can go on to the second half of this stage.

You can now allow your dog to greet other dogs without using the long line. As they greet, keep walking and then recall your dog. The first few times that your dog responds make sure that you have a really high grade reward available or make the game particularly exciting. This is a huge achievement and he deserves to be rewarded highly.

Stage three
Now that you feel confident about your dog coming away from distractions, it is time to increase the difficulty. You will now try to recall him before he gets to the other dog/distraction. Make it easy at first, calling when your dog first sees another dog at a distance and as soon as he begins to make a move, rewarding heavily when he returns to you and then allowing your dog to go and see the other one before recalling. Once again the dog gets a 'double reward'. Practise this at decreasing distances as your dog's response improves. At times you will be able to allow your dog to go off again, or you will be able to keep him with you by extending the game until the other dog is out of sight. Gradually you will be able to change the types of reward and the frequency at which they are given, so that your dog will never know what he is coming back for, be it a tasty reward, a piece of dried dog food, a game with his favourite toy or just some verbal praise from you. Good luck!

Retrieve

Some dogs love to retrieve a ball or toy. Others might chase a toy but are not interested in bringing it back, and some aren't even interested in the chase. Some dogs have been put off retrieving when, perhaps, as a puppy they were told off for retrieving a tea towel or another 'treasure' they had come across.

When a dog enjoys retrieving a ball (playing 'fetch'), it is an excellent game to play in a field or even in your garden. It is a good way of exercising your dog and making you more interesting to your dog when he is off lead.

When you are teaching the retrieve it is worth remembering that it is in fact a series of actions that you are asking for:

- *go towards the toy*
- *pick the toy up*
- *hold the toy*
- *return to the owner (still holding the toy)*
- *stop in front of the owner*
- *hold the toy until the owner asks for a drop or give*
- *drop the toy into the owner's hand (or on the ground if you prefer).*

This is actually quite a complex behaviour, especially for a dog that is not a natural retriever.

The easiest way for your dog to learn this exercise is to teach him in reverse order. So the first thing you need to teach him is the last part of the exercise – drop the toy into your hand or onto the floor.

Don't try to rush the training. It might take several sessions for your dog to progress to the complete exercise. Finish the training session before he can get bored, and come back to it at a later time.

Produce your chosen toy or article (do not push the toy into his mouth). If he takes the toy, mark it and offer a reward (so he will drop it back into your hand – don't worry if, to start with, he drops it to the floor). Initially you may need to mark and reward him for just touching it with his nose, before you begin to wait for him to open his mouth on it. If he is really not interested in holding the toy, try to make it more interesting. Run it along the floor like 'prey' for your dog to grab, hide it behind you or perhaps take a great deal of interest in it yourself. One or all of these should make the toy more appealing to your dog. You can then mark and reward him for sniffing and taking an interest in the article, and gradually ask for a little more interest before rewarding. So, reward for a couple of sniffs, then wait for a more enthusiastic sniffing or mouthing before rewarding, and soon he should be trying to take the toy into his mouth (for which he should be rewarded enthusiastically).

When he is happily taking the toy from your hand, you can put the toy on your knee or between your knees (if you are sitting down) or on the floor. All being well, he will pick it up and give it to you. Mark and reward. Break the training for a few minutes before you go back to it. Drop the toy on the floor (close to you) for a few more times until your dog is again comfortable with what is required of him, then increase the distance and he will probably happily race after it and bring it back. However, some dogs are not so confident, and if you throw the toy 20 feet away he may ignore it or chase it and then forget what the next bit is. If your dog is like this, then take it slowly and make sure you have started this exercise in a quiet environment with no distractions; then begin to increase the distance you are throwing the toy in small stages. If at any point you find the dog loses interest then take the distance back to the one he could cope with, ask him to bring the toy to you and when he does, mark, reward and finish the training session.

If you have a natural retriever you will be able to miss out most of this training, but you might still like to train him to give you the toy in your hand, saving an awful lot of bending down on your part.

If your dog is really keen to retrieve, you might occasionally ask him to wait before going to fetch the toy. (Don't ask him to wait every time or he may well decide the game is boring, and stop retrieving altogether.) This is useful for a couple of reasons. It will help him to learn some self-control and it will mean that you can prevent him from running after inappropriate objects like a child's toy or a cricket ball. If you have a dog who is the least bit reluctant to retrieve, it is probably best not to ask him to wait.

A word of caution: please make sure that any retrieve toy is suitable for your dog. If you are using a ball for instance, it should be big enough that the dog cannot swallow it or choke on it (but not so big that he can't pick it up). Never be tempted to use a stick to throw for your dog – it can easily stick in the ground and cause damage to your dog's body or mouth if he is still running when he reaches it, or it could stick in the ground when he is returning to you.

Settle

If your puppy understands the words 'settle down' it can be very valuable when he is underfoot while you are cooking, being a bit of a nuisance around the dinner table or when visitors call.

Rather than using a formal stay cue, which would imply that he should remain in one place until told to move, 'settle down' is a more relaxed cue asking that he just lie down out of the way and to indicate to him that there is nothing much going on for him to worry about.

Insight
'Settle' is a more relaxed version of 'stay'.

The best approach is to use the words 'settle down' when he just lies down quietly on his own accord, and to reward him for this. It is quite surprising how many owners will spend a large amount of time and effort actively teaching a cue, but will ignore the puppy when he does nothing and is just being quiet.

By teaching this at times when your puppy is only too happy to go and have a quiet nap, such as on his return from a walk or after he has had his dinner, you are making a positive association between the words and the action. Once he has made the connection you can put this behaviour on cue and ask for this behaviour when it is required.

Give, mine, drop, thank you!

Dogs need to be taught how to give their owners something that they would rather keep. This may be toys, bones, chews, or even that pair of socks they find so tempting. This is not as difficult as it sounds. If you can teach your dog that it is worth his while to give things back, you will find that he will choose this option.

Stages to giving up a toy:

- ▶ *Entice your dog to play a tug game, with you at one end of the toy and him at the other. Make sure it is an appropriate toy, i.e. a raggy or tuggie toy that is big enough for you both to get a good hold on.*
- ▶ *When you want your dog to give the toy back, stop pulling on the toy and stay as still as you can.*
- ▶ *Offer your dog something in exchange for the toy – this may be food or another toy.*
- ▶ *When your dog releases the toy, reward him.*
- ▶ *If you are using food as a reward give him the food, wait for him to eat it and offer the toy again for some more play time.*
- ▶ *If you are using another toy, as soon as he releases the first toy offer to play with him with the second toy.*
- ▶ *The equation in the dog's head should be: play with toy + give up toy = food or another game with a toy. From his point of view it is win, win.*
- ▶ *Play mix and match games. Sometimes your dog will get a food reward for giving up the toy, sometimes he will get another toy and sometimes he gets to play with the same toy.*
- ▶ *It is pure human invention to state that you, rather than your dog, must end up with the toy. Sometimes using that technique your dog will become more and more possessive over toys. It is much simpler and straightforward for your dog to learn that if he offers to give up his toy the reward is that he gets to keep it.*
- ▶ *As with most dog training we need to put a signal or cue on the behaviour we want to teach our dog.*
- ▶ *Choose a word that you will feel comfortable saying to your dog; some people say 'give', 'drop', 'mine' or 'thank you'. It does not matter what you choose as long as you and the rest of the family are consistent and repeat the word when your dog releases the toy.*
- ▶ *Using this technique your dog should feel happy and relaxed about giving up the toy.*

EXCHANGE IS NOT ROBBERY

Using a similar exchange technique, you can teach your dog to relinquish anything – including high resource items such as bones or chews.

Teaching your dog from puppyhood that you will exchange whatever he has got for something better will usually prevent any problems from developing. However, if this chance has been missed or your dog has developed a habit of resource guarding you will need a more specialized plan to follow. Please ask your vet for a referral to a qualified behaviour specialist.

Leave it

There will be times when you do not want your dog to chase, eat or perhaps even look at something. In fact you want him to *leave it*. The easiest way to teach your dog this skill is to teach him a verbal cue that means 'if you come away from whatever you are doing I will reward you.' Follow these simple stages, not moving on to the next stage until your dog understands the current one.

▶ *Cut up a selection of treats that your dog finds particularly tasty and put them in your pocket or somewhere out of reach of your dog.*
▶ *Have a few pieces of less inviting food, perhaps some dried dog biscuit, available as well.*
▶ *With the dog off lead (your dog needs to learn how to control himself so it is simpler to start the exercise off lead and initially in a quiet environment) have the dried food in your closed hand. It is easier if you are sitting or crouching down, because you can rest your elbow on your knee and are not tempted to pull your hand away.*
▶ *Let your dog sniff your hand; he may well try to nibble, scratch and paw at your hand to try to get the food, but hold steady*

not moving your hand, waiting for the instant his nose comes away from your hand. It is likely to be a nanosecond the first couple of times. Mark and reward with a tastier treat from your other hand. The reason for this is that when you are using the leave or off cues, you should not ask them to leave, then say 'OK you can get it now.' Leave always means 'don't touch it – you will get something better than that from me in a moment.' Think ahead – if you ask your dog to leave a chicken bone, you do not want him to think it is OK to then pick it up again after a few seconds!

▶ *Repeat this several times. Your dog should now be getting the idea that it is backing off the food in your hand that earns the reward.*

▶ *You can now start to introduce your cue word; say the word quietly just as you present your closed hand. As he backs off, mark and reward him with a tastier treat than the one he has left.*

▶ *You can now start presenting him with your open hand containing the (lower grade) treat. Be ready to close your fist if he makes a move towards it. Say your cue word (as you offer your hand) and mark and reward when he moves away, or doesn't approach your hand. It won't take long for him to learn that whether your fist is open or closed, backing off and leaving the food in your hand is what gets the reward.*

Repeat this several times until he is consistently leaving the food in your hand and is backing off in anticipation of an expected reward for doing so.

Next you will need to practise this stage in several different environments so he can generalize the behaviour.

Building on this:

Ask your dog to sit, put a treat on a chair, upturned bowl or similar – appropriate to his size – so he can see the treat. Be ready to cover the treat if your dog makes a grab for it.

As you place the treat tell him 'leave it'; uncover the treat, see if he can resist for a couple of seconds. Mark it, pick the treat up and reward with a higher-grade treat. (It is important to remove the treat before rewarding otherwise your dog could take his reward plus the original treat.)

When he is reliably leaving a treat – as above – you can progress to asking your dog to 'down', placing the treat about six inches (15 cm approx) in front of his paws.

Tell him 'leave it' and uncover the treat. Again be ready cover it (with your hand or foot) if he makes a grab for it.

Once he has ignored it for a couple of seconds, remove treat, mark and reward (as above).

Gradually place the treat closer to his paws before uncovering it. Don't rush this part of the exercise; it is important that your dog is set up for success.

The goal is to be able to place a treat on each paw, and for your dog to leave it while looking at you.

Once your dog is reliable at this stage, you can begin to upgrade the food reward you are asking him to leave, and also use some toys. You may need to go back to the beginning and build up again each time you change the food/toy you are asking him to leave.

Then we begin to progress to moving objects and unexpected challenges!

Now that he has learned to leave stationary items you need to add in some movement. Ask your dog to 'leave' as you let the food drop to the floor from a low height (no more than six inches (15 cm) from the floor initially). He is likely to move towards the food so be ready to cover the food with your foot to prevent him getting it. Start by asking him to leave low-grade rewards again and build up to higher grade rewards when he understands that leave means 'don't make a move towards the food', then mark and give a big reward for leaving.

Now begin to drop from a slightly higher position, slowly building up to throwing the food to one side, but always being ready to step in to cover the food if necessary, so he is not rewarded for taking it. When he is consistent with this, start to upgrade the treats you are asking him to leave, but going back to making it easy for him to get it right before you progress the exercise.

Next, he needs to learn that leave also means 'don't touch' when you are walking past something/someone with your dog. So once again back to boring food; place a couple of pieces on the floor, walk your dog past on lead at a distance from where he cannot reach the food, and make sure you do not use the lead to stop him getting the food. Say 'leave' and stand still, and when he stops and looks back to you, mark and reward as he returns to you. Then, gradually build up on the quality of treats you are asking him to leave, so he can learn 'leave' means don't touch it at all.

Change the locations and begin to add distractions so he has to concentrate hard on what leave means. Lots of rewards for getting it right.

Next you can practise calling him past boring food on the floor, asking a friend to stand near the food so they can cover it if he tries to get it.

Keep improving on your dog's skill until you can place a row of sausages (or whatever your dog finds irresistible) and call him past them, telling him to leave.

▶ *You are now ready to put his skill to the test in the outside world.*
▶ *Practise with food and toys when you are taking him for a walk, on lead.*

▶ *Ask him to leave something that perhaps you think he has not even seen, such as next door's cat (he has probably smelled it). If he looks at you when you say 'leave' reward him big time.*

Release

A release word is used to signal to your dog that he is free to go about his business, or collect a reward; for example, when you ask your dog to sit before removing his lead at the park, he should still remain sitting (unless he has learned that the cue to go off and play is having his lead removed). Then he can be given his release cue, such as 'OK', or 'off you go'.

Sometimes this is obvious to your dog – you may have asked him to sit and walked away from him. You then call him to you – he will know he has finished the 'sit' because he has been asked to do something else.

But what if you are training your dog to do a longer 'stay'? You ask him to sit and you walk away. You ask your dog to stay. After a period you walk back to your dog and stand beside him. After a few seconds you give your dog the release word and he knows the exercise is over.

If he is not used to being 'released' from an exercise (remember that if you have marked him to reward something he has been doing, then the marker word is the release) he may release himself. The release cue is useful for telling him his sit is over so he can go off and play now, or 'OK' he can get out of the car, or cross the road. It simply means it's OK to continue with something else.

You can introduce your release word fairly early on in training, for example, when you feed your dog and are teaching him food manners (see Chapter 5). Your release word can be used here to indicate to your dog – 'you can go ahead and eat your dinner.' The same applies for getting in and out of the car and going across roads. Make sure the word you use is clear and obvious to the dog. If your dog is sitting to have his lead removed, and you say your release cue, you may need to move off briskly and encourage your dog to go with you so he can learn what the cue means. They usually pick this up quickly, but don't expect your dog to do a ten-minute sit stay if he is really excited about playing in the park. Build up the time before release gradually, the same as for the stays, asking for very short periods initially and then gradually building up and then generalizing it.

10 THINGS TO REMEMBER

1 *Keep training sessions short and fun, with a variety of rewards to keep you and your dog motivated.*

2 *Always finish training sessions on a 'high'. Do not fail at something, get fed up and pack up. If your dog is struggling with an exercise, ask him to do something easy, or something he particularly enjoys before finishing.*

3 *Each new behaviour you teach your dog needs to be taught in at least five or six different locations for your dog to be able to generalize it.*

4 *Your dog needs to work in all these different locations with varying levels of distractions to ensure the behaviour is reliable.*

5 *The bigger the distractions, the higher the grade of reward should be.*

6 *Your dog is motivated by different rewards – dried dog food might be fine for easy behaviours at home, but is not going to be motivating in the park.*

7 *Attention is the most important part of training. Until you have your dog's attention you will not succeed in training him.*

8 *Do not nag your dog. Constantly repeating the same cue is not an effective way of obtaining behaviour.*

9 *Do not use his name as a substitute for other cues – e.g. don't say 'Rover' when you mean 'come here', or 'Rover' when you mean 'don't pull'.*

10 *Remember that your dog is not being deliberately disobedient just to annoy you. He simply does not understand what you want.*

7

....

Top ten tips

In this chapter you will learn:
- *how to understand your dog better*
- *how to read your dog's body language*
- *how to get the best out of your dog.*

---

1 Managing the environment your dog lives in is the key to stress-free dog ownership

Often the easiest way to solve some common problems is to manage the environment so that your dog is unable to perform the behaviour you do not like. If he raids the bin, move it out of reach. If he digs craters in your lawn, do not allow him unsupervised access to the garden. If he has house-training problems then you should take him outside more often, and restrict his access as described in the section on house-training (Chapter 5). If he gets overexcited at the door when visitors arrive, throw a handful of treats into the kitchen or his crate when the doorbell rings and shut the door, only allowing him access to visitors when he is calm and your guests are settled.

There are many ways that you can make your life easier and help your dog to quickly and effectively learn how to behave. Always set your dog up to succeed, thus avoiding unnecessary nagging at your dog and avoiding confusion. A common mistake is to continually tell your dog 'no' don't do this, or that, or the other, but we don't actually show our dog what we would like them to do. So managing the environment with the use of baby-gates and crates in the early stages will help to avoid this. Your dog cannot understand that, although you have told him not to go upstairs at least ten times and bring him down when he does, it means he is not allowed upstairs.

SOME OTHER HELPFUL ADVICE

▶ *If your dog pulls on the lead all the time, use a suitable head collar or training harness while you train him to walk with a loose lead.*

▶ *Feed him a good quality food and keep him fit and active. This will save you vet's bills.*

▶ *Make sure your garden is fully dog-proofed, the fence being high enough so that he can't jump over it, and there are no holes in the hedges or fence that he can get through.*

▶ *Check your dog's identity tag regularly, so that if he ever gets lost he can be returned to you quickly.*

▶ *If your dog barks at the front window, shut the door to that room.*

▶ *If your children leave toys and clothes laying on the floor your puppy will undoubtedly pick them up and run off with them. Don't blame your puppy – teach your children to be tidy!*

▶ *There will be lots of times when you need your dog to settle down, keep a low profile and not bother you. He'll be much happier and more settled if you give him a large, tasty chew or stuffed Kong to keep him occupied. Likewise, when you have to leave him alone he will be much happier with a safe, tasty chew to keep him busy.*

▶ *If you have young children and they have friends to play, your dog should be kept apart from the children, or kept under control. He may be fine with your children, but some visiting children may be afraid of dogs, get too excited and upset your dog.*

Insight
Keep children and dogs apart when unsupervised.

Just a little forethought can make things run more smoothly and relieve stress.

LITTLE AND OFTEN

Short, fun training sessions throughout the day, in a variety of situations will help your puppy to learn effectively what is required of him in everyday life. Often we are doing these training exercises without realizing it, for example, when we ask our puppy to sit for dinner or put his lead on to go in the garden. If your puppy is very excited because he knows you are going to let him off lead to 'go play' at the park, it is really worthwhile waiting for him to sit calmly just for a couple of seconds so that he can learn that calm behaviour is what gets him what he wants. Sessions should be short so that both you and your puppy do not get frustrated, and he has time to absorb what he has been learning.

Insight
    Keep training sessions short and fun.

Always try to end any training session on a positive note, and try not to train your puppy if you have had a really bad day at work or are not feeling up to it. Provide him with something like a stuffed Kong, or hide some toys and treats around the house so he has something to occupy him and then he can settle down while you can chill without feeling guilty. The short commercial breaks on the television are an ideal time to get some training done and just about the right length of time. Always have some of his dinner set aside or some treats ready in a pot and you are ready to go when the advertisements come on. If your puppy gets really excited and can't seem to stop jumping when the treat pot comes out, you will need to really work hard at rewarding calmer behaviour, and also try to reward him when he is in the position you have 'marked'. (This is useful for puppies who, as soon as they have heard their 'marker', try to mug you for their reward.) If you have a more hesitant puppy who seems unsure what is required, you will need to be more patient, use bigger rewards for smaller efforts on the way to the finished behaviour. (See 'Shaping', Chapter 1.)

SETTLE

It is really useful if you can switch your puppy 'off'. The best time to teach the 'settle' exercise is when your puppy is tired and will settle down naturally. When he does settle (relaxed down, bottom cocked to one side usually), quietly stroke him and tell him he is a good boy to 'settle' so he starts to associate the verbal cue with the behaviour. If he finds it difficult to settle, you may find it easier initially to give him a stuffed Kong, put him on lead and sit down with him like this. You can put your foot on the lead so he is able to move around but can't go rushing off. Again, praise when he is relaxed and settled.

Insight
Remember to praise your dog when he is settled and relaxed.

Once he has the idea of settling down in one area, generalize it to different locations in the house so he really gets the idea, and again when you visit friends, and even when you are out for a walk, lead on and sit down for a few moments before carrying on with your walk. A dog you can take anywhere – pub, shop, friends' homes – is a pleasure to own.

2 Join a training class

Find your local APDT member, and go along and observe a class before you join, to ensure you are happy with how it is run. Most members run different classes for dogs of all ages and standards. Training your dog with other like-minded people in a relaxed and stress-free environment is fun, and will help you perfect your handling skills and teach your dog good manners around other dogs. All trainers are different and you need to find someone you feel you will get on with.

If you are unable to attend a class, APDT members often offer one-to-one training, which is very effective, although it does not teach your dog how to behave when there are other dogs around.

Even just a single one-to-one lesson in your home could be very beneficial. The advantage of a private lesson is that you have the trainer's undivided attention and the training can be personalized to suit you and your dog.

Some dogs get too excited and stressed in a class environment and are much better with one-to-one training. A good trainer should be able to assess your dog and advise you what is appropriate if you are not sure. Likewise, some people find a class situation too nerve-wracking and are unable to cope if their puppy is not as quick as the puppy next to them, or if their puppy appears to lack concentration.

If you are interested in working your dog in any of the many disciplines now available, be it gun dog work, obedience, agility, showing (to name a few), a good grounding in basic exercises using reward-based, motivational training will stand you in good stead whatever you decide to do. Dog sports are gaining in popularity all the time and most participants who start off by taking their dog to a pet dog training class, find that they really enjoy training their dog and go on to progress the basics they have learned or branch off into other dog-related sports.

Well-meaning friends, neighbours and even complete strangers are always keen to give you advice on how you should train your dog. This advice can often be totally inappropriate (e.g. 'hit him on the nose with a rolled up newspaper', 'rub his nose in it', 'your dog is being dominant', 'you must show him who's boss') and will frequently not help at all or can cause other problems. It is unwise to heed this type of advice if you want to avoid exacerbating the problem at hand. APDT members have to keep themselves abreast of the latest, scientific, proven methods of training, so choose carefully the trainer you wish to advise you; after all, it is your precious pet you are dealing with. Never let a trainer or anyone else take your dog away to reprimand it or 'sort it out', and don't feel you have to let someone bully you into doing as they advise. If you are uncomfortable with anything someone suggests, simply say thank you and goodbye!

DOG TRAINING IS FUN

People acquire dogs for a huge variety of reasons, whether it is to have a companion, a show dog or a friend for another pet. The best way of building a strong bond with your dog is to spend time training and playing with him. Walks are an ideal time to train and play with your dog.

Insight
Walks are an ideal time to do some training.

Rather than have your dog mooching disconsolately behind you on walks, paying no attention to you, interact with him so he finds you fun to be with and enjoys your company. This will mean he is keen to return to you when you ask him to.

If your dog loves to chase toys and bring them back to you, then it is easy to play with him. If he is not toy motivated, then thickly sliced sausages can be thrown or scattered and hidden for your dog to find. This will satisfy his hunting instincts and make you much more interesting to be with.

3 Base your relationship with your dog on mutual trust and respect

Your dog should look at you for guidance and support without having all his natural enthusiasms curbed. For instance, when your dog is going through his adolescent phase it would be unfair and very frustrating for you if he spends every moment of his walk seeking out other dogs and completely ignoring you. If you work hard on basic obedience, and use good management techniques, it is possible to train your dog to only run off to play with your permission. If you can find another dog owner with a dog of similar age and size (someone from your training class, perhaps) you could meet up for a walk and play session. If you train your dog to sit and look at you, and then reward him with a 'go play' cue, he will learn to seek your permission before going off to play. Dogs need a certain amount of freedom to just be dogs – to sniff about and interact with other dogs. If you have a well-trained dog you will be able to trust him.

The breeder may have advised that your breed of dog should never be let off lead, or you may just be terrified that your dog will run away if you allow him any freedom. If you build up a good relationship with your dog and train a reliable recall there is no reason why your dog should not enjoy his freedom in areas where it is safe to do so.

Your relationship with your dog should be a matter of mutual trust and respect, not a battle of wills.

Insight
Your relationship should be based on mutual trust and respect.

Remember you are rewarding your dog for good behaviour, not trying to bribe him into doing something. It is unrealistic to expect your dog to do everything just for 'love' – we need to give him a reason to love us first! The only way to achieve this is by effective training.

4 Always have a few dog treats in your pocket

Treats make an effective reward, being quick and easy to use. The more you reward your dog, especially when teaching a new exercise, the more your dog will want to perform that exercise. You never know when an opportunity may arise to reinforce a good behaviour, so be prepared.

In early training, whenever your dog does something good – reward him! When he comes back to you quickly, reward him; praise him when he is obviously on the way back to you so he knows something good is about to happen. If he is walking beautifully beside you on a loose lead, use the opportunity to show him that you really appreciate this. You can use treats in an emergency to distract your dog from things such as fox poo, other dogs, people, joggers or bicycles. If your timing is good you can distract your dog, reward him for something you would like him to do, and pop him back on the lead before he has the chance to roll in the fox poo, or chase the jogger.

If your dog prefers toys, carry a small toy with you and use that instead. Some dogs enjoy both and this gives you more scope for variety.

---

5 Remember – your dog is not being 'naughty', he is just being a dog

Most of the behaviours your dog performs that you do not like are usually normal dog behaviours. Biting, barking, hunting, fighting, weeing, pooing, digging, jumping up, playing, stealing food, chewing, all these behaviours are normal to your dog. Because we like our dogs to live as part of our family, we have to teach them how we would like them to behave – by managing the environment they live in and allowing them an outlet for certain innate behaviours.

Puppies need to learn to inhibit their bite, so if in later life your dog is ever put in a position where he has no alternative but to bite, he has learned that no pressure is required on human flesh to cause harm! (See the section in Chapter 5 on bite inhibition.)

The reason for excessive barking needs to be identified, then avoided and/or managed so that it does not cause a nuisance to others.

If you are unsure how your dog may react around livestock you need to have it on a lead and under control. A farmer has every right to shoot a dog he believes is worrying his livestock. Always be sensible, and if in doubt keep your dog on a lead.

Early appropriate socialization with other dogs, adults and children and carefully controlled play with other puppies and dogs should help ensure that your dog knows how to interact sensibly with humans and dogs and so avoid conflict with other dogs and display fear behaviours around humans.

Puppies – and some re-homed dogs – need vigilant house-training. This does not happen by itself. You need to make sure your puppy is given the opportunity to go outside often enough and rewarded when he does. Do not punish him if he has an accident indoors; that was your fault, not his, because you were not watching him closely enough.

Your dog's character traits and his behaviour will often be closely linked to his breed. Border Collies herd, Retrievers carry things around in their mouth, Hounds follow scents, Terriers go down holes after rats and rabbits (although this should not be encouraged as it could be dangerous), guarding breeds bark at strangers, fighting breeds play roughly (although you shouldn't encourage this either), lapdogs may not enjoy going for a ten-mile hike. With careful training you can modify and redirect your dog's behaviour, but you cannot extinguish it completely.

Always consider what you are trying to teach your dog. If you attempt to change your dog's behaviour by using force and coercion you will destroy your relationship and may actually encourage your dog to return force with force. He could thereby develop a deep mistrust of people. If you are having problems, always seek advice from your vet and get a referral to a behaviourist if needed.

---

6 Crate train your puppy

If you are thinking of getting a puppy or already have a young dog, appropriate use of a crate is a wonderful tool. Older dogs can also be crate-trained if necessary. As far as a puppy is concerned a crate is simply a den, a comfortable safe place to retire to for a sleep, and a bolt hole if life gets too much. Of course, your puppy should not be left in a crate all day.

THE CRATE

There is a misconception among the general public that it is somehow cruel to shut a puppy in a crate, but if introduced correctly a puppy does not see it like that. Occasionally, some puppies cannot settle in a cage and obviously it would be cruel to insist if they are very distressed. Some puppies are very unhappy when they are first left alone at night, and sometimes it is worth taking the crate and your puppy into your bedroom initially and gradually move it out to where you want it to be.

The vast majority of puppies will not soil in their crate. This can be of immense help when house-training, because you can take your puppy straight outside when he wakes from a nap. If you allow him to fall asleep anywhere he will probably move and relieve himself as soon as he wakes up, wherever that may be; if he has been crated he will whine to get out to go and relieve himself. If you cannot supervise your puppy, then pop him in his crate.

If you are leaving a young puppy in a crate overnight, you should put a tray with a turf of grass in the crate (separate from his bedding), so if he can't wait for you to come downstairs to let him out, he has somewhere to toilet.

The crate is a safe place for your puppy to go when you are out.

Insight

A crate is a safe place for your puppy to go when you have visitors and when you are vacuuming or washing the kitchen floor, eating meals or the children have their toys spread all over the floor.

If you go away to visit friends or take your puppy on holiday, his crate will provide a safe, portable home and he will not cause you embarrassment if he has an accident, so you and your puppy will be welcome anywhere.

It is advisable to keep your puppy crated when you cannot supervise him, until he is past the chewing stage. You may have to buy a larger crate, but it will be worth it. If your dog ever injures himself or has an operation that necessitates rest, it will be extremely useful to be able to keep him in his crate. Trying to rest a dog is virtually impossible if they have access to the entire house.

You can now buy soft, light, collapsible tent-like crates for your dog, which are very portable and immensely useful.

If you have an estate car, a crate in the back keeps your dog comfortable and safely confined. It also leaves room around the crate for luggage and shopping, Incidentally, all dogs by law should be confined in some way in the car. A loose dog is very dangerous in an accident and many people have been injured, sometimes fatally, by flying dogs (let alone the injuries caused to dogs). An unrestrained dog in the back seat is in as much danger as a child who has not been belted in. A crate, a good dog guard, or a dog car harness is essential if you have your dog in the car with you. If you own one of the herding breeds that are inclined to bark when cars are whizzing past, then a crate with a cover over it can block out the view and put a stop to this particular behaviour.

---

7 Learn as much as you can about dog behaviour

If you are interested enough to read this book, you might like to learn more about dog behaviour and training. A good start would be a subscription to one of the monthly magazines published for dog owners. These are readily available at your local newsagent and are packed full of articles on dog behaviour, training and health as well as all the latest news concerning dogs.

Your local library should have a good selection of books on dogs. From reading this book you will understand how kind, fair and effective training works and how you can teach your dog to be a well-mannered, happy family pet without using force or confrontation. Not all books adhere to these principles; many still advocate coercive methods, the use of check/choke chains and other unnecessary equipment. When you read books, do not assume that because 'experts' wrote them that they will give you the best, most up-to-date advice. However, with a discerning mind it can be fascinating to read some of the more old-fashioned training books.

There is a wealth of good books and videos available. Look at the recommended reading list in 'Taking it further' for some good ideas on getting started.

Observing other dogs and their owners can also teach you a lot. Compare a happy, carefree, obedient dog with an out-of-control hooligan. How do the owners behave? Do they appear confident or unsure? Are they constantly nagging their dogs? Do they play with their dogs? Studying the behaviour of owners and their dogs can be a real eye-opener, and it is always easier to see where someone else may be going wrong than to see your own mistakes!

8 Learn to read your dog's body language

It may sound obvious, but dogs do not communicate with words. They do not speak English or any other human language. They communicate using subtle body language and it can help your relationship with them enormously if you take a little time to learn what dog language means.

Insight

It is important to understand what your dog's body language means.

We try very hard to teach them some of our words and so it would be nice if we could understand what they were trying to tell us. Dogs use their whole bodies, mouth, eyes, ears, tail and posture to convey their feelings, both physical and mental, and more and more research into this fascinating subject is going on all the time. There have been some great books published on this subject. (Look at the recommended reading list in 'Taking it further'.)

Because dogs come in such a huge variety of shapes and sizes, it can be more difficult to read the signals of some breeds. Tail docking is a good example. It can be very hard, if not impossible, to work out what a docked dog's tail is telling you and it is also very difficult for another dog to interpret. Thankfully it is now illegal for the majority of puppies to have their tails docked (in the UK at least), but for the time being there are still plenty of adult dogs with docked tails.

The following is a very brief description of the most common body language you may observe in your dog.

THE MOUTH

A dog's mouth can be very expressive, and convey all the emotions he is feeling at that moment. If you pick up on the signals your puppy gives you early enough you can defuse a great deal of the behaviour about to be shown.

Mouth open
Mouth relaxed and slightly open, tongue may be visible. The sign of a happy, contented dog.

Mouth open, panting with the mouth pulled back is a very anxious dog.

Mouth closed
A tightly closed mouth accompanied by a turning away of the head means, 'I'm a bit unsure' and is a pacifying gesture. A closed mouth with a slight forward lean of the ears and head and a forward gaze means, 'I'm watching something of interest over there.' Standing very still with a closed mouth and ears erect means, 'I am listening

to something.' It is a bit like when we stand still to decide what to do next.

Lips

Lips curled to expose some teeth means, 'Don't come any closer.' This is a threat, often used after more subtle signals have been used and failed. It usually works extremely well at getting other dogs and humans to move away.

Lips curled to expose major teeth, mouth partly open and nose area wrinkled is the threat that means, 'I mean it, if you do not go away I will bite you.'

Lips curled to expose all the teeth and gums above the front teeth with very noticeable wrinkles above the nose is the ultimate. 'This is your last chance, if you don't back off I really will bite.'

Figure 7.1 A dog's various mouth expressions.

Grinning

There are certain breeds of dog that 'smile' and it can be a 'submissive' gesture used when you are greeted by your dog. Many people mistake a 'smile' for an aggressive display and nothing could be further from the truth. Dalmatians, dobermans and many terriers all are known to be 'smilers'.

EYES

Eye contact
Dogs do not naturally view direct eye contact as a pleasant experience. In the wild they would view a direct stare as a threat. However, a puppy will soon learn that eye contact combined with a pleasant facial expression from the owner and a treat is a very rewarding experience. This is something that should be trained from puppyhood, as children are all prone to look a dog in the eye. Liking eye contact can also make a nervous dog a bit more confident. Never stare your dog down in anger, as this will make him very wary of eye contact with anyone.

Staring
A direct stare at another dog is often a threat. It often happens in a training class situation that two dogs will stare (often referred to as 'eyeballing') at each other and if this is not interrupted by distracting them and turning their heads away, it may well lead to trouble. Off lead you will often see two dogs standing, staring at each other. Usually one dog will back down by turning his head away.

Showing the whites of the eye
A dog which shows the whites of its eyes is usually a very fearful dog that will bite because of the position he is in.

Enlarged pupils
A dog in a highly aroused state will have dilated pupils.

THE TAIL

We have all probably heard people say, 'He didn't mean it, he was wagging his tail!' There are many different ways of wagging a tail and they all signify different things – interpretation depends on carriage of tail and speed of wag.

9 Make it your dog's responsibility to stay in touch with you on walks

Very few dogs will stay in sight all the time on walks. They get their noses down on wonderful scents and disappear into the undergrowth; they will chase rabbits, squirrels, pheasants and sometimes deer. (This should never be encouraged as it can be dangerous for your dog and the animal it is chasing.) They may go and say hello to every other dog and human that they meet. Most owners panic immediately their dog goes out of sight and quickly call them back, usually with no response. They then keep on calling until the dog eventually returns from his adventures, tired but happy with his run.

This means that all the time your dog is away he is secure in the knowledge that you are close by and will wait for his return. Of course, if you get angry and punish your dog when he returns your recall will get even slower as your dog learns that coming back is not a pleasant experience.

Your dog needs to be a bit worried that he might lose you on a walk, not the other way around. If you are unpredictable and keep your dog on his toes he will return more quickly. When your dog runs off ahead of you along a path, try turning and going in the opposite direction without a word. When your dog comes bounding up to you, praise him and give him a treat. You can also hide from your dog when he is not looking, keeping quiet so that he comes looking for you.

This is best done when your puppy is a youngster and still unsure of himself – you should make sure that you can see your puppy, even if he can't see you. When he is first learning this game you do not want him to panic. However, it will also work with older dogs if you take them to an unfamiliar place and play the hiding game.

If you constantly tell your dog where you are he knows that he can carry on with whatever is occupying him, safe in the knowledge that you are waiting for him. On familiar territory he may also know his way home, or where the car is parked.

You could also have a problem getting your dog back if you are too free and easy with the rewards. Dogs work better if they don't know what good things will come their way when they come back to you. If your dog knows what a recall means, reward the fastest, quickest responses or play a game with him when he is extra quick at coming back. If you reward him with much more than praise and a pat when he comes back to you after ten minutes, then that is what you are training him to do.

10 Reward, reward, reward!

We often ignore dogs when they are being good because they are not bothering us, but we are missing golden opportunities to teach our dogs some important lessons. We are also increasing the chances of him doing something we don't want him to; just to gain your attention.

When your puppy greets a dog nicely and is calm around other dogs, praise and reward him. Don't just take it for granted that your dog knows how to have manners around other dogs, because he does not. If he plays with rough dogs he learns to play rough and some dogs just cannot cope with this type of play, so reinforce all the nice behaviour around other dogs. Be careful, however, if you are using food rewards for this. Simply throwing a treat to your dog could cause a fight over the treat. Check with the owner of the other dog – can they both have a treat? Or better still, 'mark' the calm behaviour and reward your dog when he returns to you.

When you are eating your meals and your puppy is lying quietly (before he learns the art of begging at the table), go over to where he is lying down and praise him quietly.

If you are standing talking to a friend and your dog is sitting quietly by your side then keep slipping him the odd treat without saying anything to him, carry on your conversation and your puppy will learn to sit and let you get on with what you need to do while he is a shining example of how a dog should behave.

Insight

Never miss out on opportunities to reward your dog for the right behaviour.

10 THINGS TO REMEMBER

1 You can manage the environment to avoid your dog having the opportunity to behave inappropriately.

2 If you decide to take your puppy or dog to a training class, be sure to go and watch the class before signing up. Make sure that they are teaching in a way you would like to train your dog.

3 Dogs need to have freedom to run and play, but teach your dog to ask for 'permission' before going so you can check it is safe for him to do so.

4 Always remember to carry some type of reward with you – toy and/or food. Just because you are not in a 'training session' does not mean that your dog is not learning. If you see something good, reward it.

5 Try to remember that dogs do not have 'good' behaviour and 'bad' behaviour. They have dog behaviour. Some of it we like and some of it we don't. The behaviour we like is rewarded and so will increase, the behaviour we don't like is ignored and so will decrease.

6 Crate training can be a useful tool when house-training, and also gives your puppy a safe haven when he needs one.

7 It will help you to understand your dog if you find out as much as possible about his breed (mix of breed or type). This will help you understand what traits he may have.

8 Learn to 'read' your dog's body language so you are aware of when he is feeling worried and can take appropriate action to help him.

9 Interact with your dog when you are out for walks – this is not a time to be chatting on your phone. You never know what might be around the corner.

10 Remember to reinforce your dog for doing nothing – do not take it for granted that he will remain settled quietly at home while you get on with other things.

8

....

Clicker training

In this chapter you will learn:
- *the history of clicker training*
- *how to start with the clicker*
- *what you can do with the clicker.*

_____

The history of the clicker

Reward-based, motivational training has been around for many years but methods were still compulsive. For example, the dog was physically made to sit and then rewarded. Gradually we have seen a change to a much more gentle, fun-based and effective way of obtaining the behaviours we want from our dogs. While the training method in this book has concentrated on those gentle, fun and effective methods, i.e. the food lure/reward method, we cannot ignore the emergence of the clicker in dog training that has happened over the last 20 or so years.

Many training instructors now run their training classes exclusively using clickers to help owners train their dogs. Each owner is provided with a clicker and when the dog has done something right, he is clicked and rewarded. (Refer to the following section on clicker training.)

Although clicker training is a comparatively new concept in dog training, it has been used for many years in training other types of animal. As far back as the 1930s, animal behaviour experts were experimenting with clickers, known then as 'crickets', and in 1951 Professor B. F. Skinner produced a paper, 'How to Teach Animals', in which he described the use of a clicker. From the 1940s to the present day the clicker has been used to train many types of animal, including 140 species of birds, dolphins, horses and at least one fish, crab and bull!

However, it wasn't until the 1980s that Karen Pryor, who started using a clicker while training marine mammals, introduced the clicker to dog trainers. In her insightful book *Don't Shoot the Dog* she describes how the clicker method can help train any creature, from people to dogs. Since then there have been many books and videos on how to use a clicker for training your dog. With correct instructions, you too can train your dog using a clicker. For more information, refer to 'Taking it further' for book ideas.

An introduction to clicker training

Clicker training is one of the most effective and enjoyable methods available. Based on sound, scientific principles, this tool will allow you to communicate with your dog and train him to do practically any action you choose and which he is physically capable of carrying out.

Insight
The clicker allows you to effectively communicate with your dog.

WHAT IS A CLICKER?

A 'clicker' (from which the method is named) is a small plastic box containing a piece of flexible steel. When pressed at one end, it makes a distinctive 'click, click' sound that can be taught to have meaning for your dog. Throughout this book, when we refer to 'marking' the behaviour, a clicker acts as a marker.

HOW DOES IT WORK?

After a few repetitions, your dog learns that the sound of the clicker means he's done the right thing and that a reward – food, play or some other reward that he finds motivating – is on its way.

Insight
> The sound of the clicker is always followed by a reward.

HOW WILL MY DOG UNDERSTAND WHAT IT MEANS?

Your dog will make the association between the clicker and goodies by repetition and reward. The sound of the clicker marks the dog's action as being right, a little like putting a tick next to a correct sum on a page.

Insight
> The clicker marks the action to indicate to your dog he has done right.

WHY IS THE CLICKER TRAINING SO EFFECTIVE?

It is always positive and highly accurate. You can give clear information to your dog about his actions up close, or from a distance, without your feelings about your stressful day or the weather being expressed, as they often are in your voice. The clicker predicts that a reward will follow actions you want – simply ignore actions that you don't.

Insight
> The clicker conveys clear information to your dog.

Clicker training

Initially the 'click' will mean nothing to your dog – it is just one more sound in a noisy world. But it is a unique sound and if each time your dog hears the click he is given a reward, it will soon become a very important sound.

The 'click' signals to the dog that he is correct; whatever he has done is what you were looking for. It may be that it is only part of the behaviour that you are after, but it will let the dog know he is on the right track – he is getting there.

Consistency is very important when training your dog, never more so than when using a clicker. A 'click' is **always** followed by a reward.

There are different ways of introducing the clicker (some trainers refer to it as 'charging' the clicker). The method given below, by asking for your dog's attention, is probably one of the best.

When introducing the clicker, muffle the sound. Put it behind your back, in your pocket or somewhere similar. Most dogs are fine with the noise, but a very sound-sensitive dog may not enjoy it. Have it muffled for a few clicks and then gradually work to its normal level (behind you, muffled or in a pocket; behind you unmuffled; and then held in your hand in the way you are going to use it).

If your dog does not like the sound you can use a 'click' word (also referred to as a marker word) instead. Even if your dog is happy with the clicker you should also have a 'click' word. A 'click' word works in exactly the same way as a clicker – it is a short word that is used to mark the behaviour you want – 'good', 'yes' or similar. The secret to the click word is, again, that it is always followed by a reward. The word must be short, for there is no point trying to mark the exact behaviour you want by saying, for instance, 'wonderful!' By the time you have finished the word the dog could be in a different position, e.g. you have asked your dog to sit, he sits, you say wonder .... and before you can finish the dog has got up. As far as he is concerned he is being rewarded for a quick sit and jump up again, or for the moving around. Not what you want! Because the word is always followed by a reward, it must be a word that is not used in normal interaction with the dog; not, for example, 'good dog'. Hopefully you are telling your dog he is a good dog on a fairly frequent basis, but you are not rewarding him every time you say it. So the word needs to be unique, and kept for marking the behaviour you require.

- *A clicker should never be used near a dog's (or anyone else's) ear.*
- *Click just once for the required behaviour.*
- *A click is always followed by a reward.*
- *A clicker is not a remote control – you do not need to point it at your dog.*
- *A clicker is not a toy. It is very tempting (especially for children) to click, click, click but in this way you will totally change the meaning of the clicker. Instead of meaning 'yes, you got it right, a reward is on its way' it will become just another noise in your dog's world.*
- *If you click at the wrong time – tough, get it right next time. Even if you click at the wrong time your dog must be rewarded otherwise the clicker will lose its effectiveness.*
- *A clicker becomes associated with reward (very often food), so be careful that your dog does not take the clicker. If he swallows it, it will be an expensive vet bill!*
- *If your dog does the required behaviour, click and reward. If he doesn't then you just don't click – simple. Once he understands the clicker he will be working very hard to get that click!*

INTRODUCING ('CHARGING') THE CLICKER

- *Prepare some small tasty high-grade treats, (sausage, cheese, chicken or liver cake are generally favourites).*
- *Say your dog's name in a happy voice.*

- As soon as he looks at you, click and give a reward.
- Repeat this three or four times.
- Soon, your dog will start to understand the meaning of the clicker and will react to the sound, thinking, 'Great, where's my treat?'

You will also have started to teach him to pay attention to you when you say his name. Now you are ready to move on to other exercises and tasks, including an explanation of how the clicker is used when teaching an exercise.

SIT

- Keep quiet, and show your dog you have a food treat in your hand. Put it on his nose, right up close. Now lift your hand up and back, so he has to look right up to follow your fingers. The movement of him looking upwards like this causes a physical chain reaction – his rear end has to go down.
- Suddenly your dog is sitting! As soon as his bottom hits the ground, click, and then give your dog the treat. It is essential that you click the very moment that your dog's bottom reaches the ground.
- Repeat this a few times. (If your dog's front legs come off the ground, your hand is probably too high.)
- Now you can say the word 'sit' just before you move the food lure. When he sits, click and reward. In a matter of minutes you have taught your dog a verbal request to sit, plus a really effective hand signal. Congratulations!
- Now, you need to phase out the food lure. With no food in your hand, ask your dog to sit. If he does so, click immediately, then give a food treat. If your dog does not sit when asked, help him with the hand signal, then reward for good efforts.
- Practise until your dog's sits are really quick and totally reliable by asking your dog to sit before he gets anything in life he likes, such as having his dinner, having his lead put on, being let out into the garden. It's his way of saying please and thank you.

AND MORE

The clicker is an excellent way of telling your dog he has got it right when he is working at a distance from you. For example, your dog may be about 20 feet away from you and you ask him to 'down' (after he has learned the behaviour, of course). You click when he goes down so he understands that he has done what you want, but he can then come back to you for the reward.

It is a good way of getting your dog to experiment with behaviours. A classic game is '101 things to do with a box' developed by Karen Pryor. This is a great game for any dog, but it is especially useful for a dog who has been trained using old-fashioned, coercive methods where he has had to wait to be told what to do, and has been punished for deviating from that behaviour. It will encourage him to think for himself. If your dog has been trained using coercive methods then it may take him a while to understand that he can try new things – be patient. It is not his fault that he has been trained not to think for himself. The aim of the exercise is to get him to interact with the box, ideally to step into it.

Get a box and cut the sides down to about 3 inches (8 centimetres) in height (or less if you have a very small dog). Have your clicker and rewards ready and put the box on the floor. Dogs react differently but most will at least look at the box; if so, click and treat. If the dog walks towards the box or passes by it, click and treat. Throw the treat near to the box and click as the dog moves towards it. Reward again. If he steps into the box, click and reward him from your hand. If your dog ignores the box don't be tempted to pat the box, point or similar. Just be patient. This is a new game for your dog – he doesn't yet understand it.

Click any foot movement towards the box. If the first time you play this your dog loses interest before stepping into the box, no problem. Just pick up the box and keep it for another session. The more he gets used to being clicked and rewarded the more likely he is to progress next time.

To encourage your dog to step into the box you can throw treats into the box. Don't worry if he doesn't immediately pick them up – when he does venture into the box he will get multiple treats!

If your dog does something you like, e.g. looks cute, walks backwards or even just lies down if you are having problems with that behaviour – click and treat. Initially your dog will probably not understand what he has been rewarded for but after a few repetitions, even if they are quite a time apart, he *will* understand what he is being rewarded for. Once he starts offering the behaviour you can put it on cue.

Insight

He understands the cue, when he consistently offers the behaviour each time you give the cue.

Once he understands the cue, i.e. when you give him the cue and he consistently offers the behaviour every time, then he is only rewarded when you cue the behaviour, and not at other times.

If you have access to the internet you will find lots of articles on clicker training there. Have a look and get some great ideas. There are also books that deal exclusively with clicker training ideas.

10 THINGS TO REMEMBER

1   *A clicker (or click/marker word) is an excellent way to effectively communicate with your dog.*

2   *The clicker lets him know exactly what he has done that has earned him the reward.*

3   *A click is **always** followed by a reward – the clicker must never lie.*

4   *Only click once to mark the behaviour.*

5   *The clicker is not a remote control – you do not need to point it at your dog.*

6   *You can use the clicker to 'capture' behaviours that your dog performs naturally, enabling you to put it on cue.*

7   *You can 'shape' a behaviour by clicking and rewarding closer and closer approximations to the final result.*

8   *Never click near your dog's (or anyone's) ear.*

9   *The clicker is best used to mark the correct behaviour, not to get your dog's attention.*

10 *Clicker training can help an anxious dog dare to try something new and think for itself, and in this way can improve his confidence.*

9

Where to find a puppy

In this chapter you will learn:
- *what to look for when choosing a breeder*
- *what to look for when choosing a puppy*
- *the places to avoid.*

Deciding on getting a puppy is a big step to take, especially if this is your first puppy. Among other things, you should take into account the time you can devote to your puppy, how to train him, the size of dog that will suit your home and car, the grooming requirements, how much exercise he will need, whether to get a male or female, the cost of food, equipment, veterinary treatment and boarding kennels; and particular consideration should be given to which breed will suit your lifestyle.

> **Insight**
> Getting a puppy is a big step.

If you decide on a pedigree puppy, you are fairly sure of knowing what you are getting; you'll know how big he will be, how long the coat will be, the breed's characteristics, how much exercise he will need, and how much it will cost you to feed him. With a cross-breed or mongrel you may have no idea of his eventual size, what his coat will look like, or whether he will show any breed characteristics that have been passed down from his parents. This may or may not be a problem for you, but is something that you and your family should bear in mind.

Where to start

If you decide to get a puppy and have chosen the breed that all the family have agreed upon, a good starting point is to contact the appropriate breed club. All breeds registered with the Kennel Club have breed clubs. They can provide useful information about the characteristics of the breed and what is required for its general care and welfare. They may also be able to put you in touch with breeders in your part of the country. See 'Taking it further' for contact details of the Kennel Club.

You can visit Discover Dogs, which is held at Earls Court, London every November and at Crufts, held every March at the NEC, Birmingham. Here you will be able to see many of the different breeds registered with the Kennel Club. Check with the Kennel Club or appropriate breed club whether your breed will be in attendance on the day you are planning to visit. You'll be able to speak to owners and breeders who can tell you all there is to know about the breed(s) you may be considering, both the good and not so good points. They might be able to give you details of someone who has bought a puppy from them so you can find out more about what the breed is like to live with.

Whether you are looking for a pedigree pup, a cross-breed or a mongrel, finding the right puppy that has been reared correctly and has started socialization is essential.

Insight
It is worth waiting for a well-bred and reared puppy.

It may take some time to find a good breeder who rears puppies in 'ideal' conditions and has a litter for sale, so be patient. When you consider that you will have your puppy for probably ten to 15 years, it is well worth getting it right. Try to see as many litters as possible and talk to as many breeders as possible. If you arrange to visit a number of breeders there is less risk of falling in love with the first puppy you see!

RE-HOMING CENTRES

Sometimes, unwanted litters are left at re-homing centres. National re-homing centres are the RSPCA, the Dogs Trust and the Blue Cross. There are lots of other well-known re-homing centres around the country, some that are independently run, and many of which have charitable status. If you are not sure where you should go, speak to the Kennel Club, your vet or vet's receptionist who will have details of re-homing centres in your area. Most of the breed clubs operate their own rescue/re-homing service, so if you want a particular breed you might want to check with them. Generally they have older dogs, but occasionally they have puppies waiting for re-homing, or a pregnant bitch they are caring for. Please refer to 'Taking it further'.

What to look for

You may not be able to see the sire (father) but it is essential that you see the dam (mother) with her puppies. If the breeder gives an excuse as to why the dam is not available – she's being taken for a walk, for example – walk away! When you do see the dam, watch her temperament while she is on her own with her puppies and when you pick up one of them. If she appears stressed or shows any sign of aggression, move on to the next breeder on your list. Any signs of aggression from the dam can be passed on to the puppy.

Insight
It is essential that you see the mother with her puppies.

Ask questions about the parents. How old are the dam and sire? Neither should be any younger than one year old. Has the dam previously had a litter? If so, when was it? Bitches should not be bred from in consecutive seasons.

Ideally the puppies should be reared in the home so they can become accustomed to the sights, sound and smells of everyday household appliances and the hustle and bustle of people coming and going. This will make life much easier when the puppy makes the transition from the breeder to his new home. If the puppy is reared in an outside kennel he won't get the necessary benefits of socialization and the stimulation that a puppy reared in the home will have. Even if the puppies are kept in kennels they should be allowed some time in the home during the day so they become accustomed to household noises, so ask how often the puppies are allowed indoors and how much time the breeder and other people spend with them. Puppies that are devoid of human contact at this stage of their life may be shy of people later on. If the puppy is reared in a kennel, make sure it is dry, warm and clean, and is in a good state of repair.

There should be plenty of toys for the puppies to play with that will stimulate them and help them develop mentally and physically. Also watch how the puppies play and interact with each other as well as the dam. This is a very important part of how puppies learn to behave as dogs.

If possible, go and see a litter at three weeks of age when their eyes and ears open and they start moving around. See them each week or two weeks until they are allowed to come home. During this time, the breeder should start socializing them with as many different experiences as is sensibly possible, starting with gentle handling at just a few days of age. This will cause mild stress, which will help the puppy deal with more stressful situations later in life. The breeder should play an important part in starting the socialization process that will help the puppy cope with life when he goes to his new home.

Apart from handling the puppies, the breeder should ensure they meet as many different people of all ages as is possible. For example, if the breeder is a lady make sure she has invited men to handle the puppies, and has also allowed children of different ages to do the same. The puppies can even be taken out in the car for short journeys.

HEREDITARY AILMENTS

If you are buying a pedigree puppy, you should be aware of the hereditary ailments of your chosen breed. Check that the sire and dam have been tested for those ailments by asking to see the veterinarian's or Animal Heath Trust certificate.

Insight

Make sure the parents have been tested for hereditary conditions.

Ideally, the breeder should also have the certificates of previous generations, but some tests are fairly new so this is not always possible. Results of some tests are shown on the pedigree. This will not guarantee the puppy won't develop the ailments later in life, but it reduces the risk. Some hereditary ailments, like deafness and Collie Eye Anomaly (CEA) for example, can be tested for in puppies when they are six or seven weeks old, so make sure this has been done.

Ask the ages of the sire and dam. Many hereditary ailments may not show for 12 months; others won't show until the dog is two years or even older. Many medium size and large breeds can suffer from a hereditary ailment called hip dysplasia, and the parents and past generations should have been 'hip scored'. Each breed that suffers from this ailment has an average hip score so, when doing your research into breeds you like, check if they suffer from hip dysplasia, find out what the average hip score is for that breed, and then ask the breeder to show you the hip scores for the parents. The scores range from 0 to 100; the lower the score, the better the hips. Ensure the score is well below the mean average for that breed.

Insight

Hip score should be well below mean average for the breed.

You can find more details of the hereditary problems and the tests available via the Kennel Club, breed club or Animal Health Trust.

BREEDING AND SALE OF DOGS ACT

Under the Breeding and Sale of Dogs Act anyone who breeds more than five litters a year must be licensed by the Local Authority. The premises are inspected annually by an independent vet, so if the breeder you intend to buy a puppy from breeds more than five litters a year, ask to see the licence. As well as other restrictions, this bans the mating of bitches under 12 months of age and on consecutive seasons. It also bans the sale of puppies under the age of eight weeks. This Act only applies to licensed breeders.

WHAT AGE TO BUY?

If the breeder is not licensed they can sell puppies younger than eight weeks old, but there is a fine line between the essential learning period when the puppy learns how to behave like a dog by playing and interacting with its siblings and dam, and going to a new home. Buy a puppy that is too young and he will miss out on those early learning benefits that only his mother can teach him, and that he acquires by playing with his litter mates. Buy one that's too old and it will miss out on the 'critical' socialization period in his new home.

The dam should have been fed on a good quality, nutritious diet before and during pregnancy and while lactating. This will give her puppies a good, healthy start to life. Also ask what the puppies have been fed during weaning and what solid food they are fed on now. The breeder should give you a diet sheet when you collect your puppy, usually with a small bag of their present diet.

If you intend to change your puppy's diet, give him a few weeks to settle into his new home first, as too many changes all at once may stress him, resulting in a severe bout of diarrhoea. Then change his diet gradually over a few days. For example, feed 75 per cent of the original diet and 25 per cent of the new diet; the next day feed

50 per cent of the original diet and 50 per cent of the new diet. The next day feed 25 per cent of the original diet and 75 per cent of the new diet, until finally you feed 100 per cent of the new diet.

CHECK OUT THE PUPPY

Once you have decided on the litter from which you are going to choose your puppy, check out the puppies to ensure they don't have any discharge from eyes, nose, ears or bottom. Their skin should not be dry or flaky and their coats should be clean. Make sure the puppies and dam have been wormed and that the dam and sire are up to date with their inoculations. Worming puppies should start when they are four weeks of age and thereafter every two weeks until 12 weeks of age (or as directed by your vet). An overly fat puppy tummy and smelly breath is a sign that your chosen puppy could be infested with worms.

If buying a Kennel Club registered puppy, when you collect him, expect to go home with a receipt of purchase, the puppy's pedigree, a diet sheet, some food and an insurance that covers your puppy's health for six weeks. If the puppy is a specific breed but the parents are not Kennel Club registered, you won't be able to register him as a pedigree, but it would be reasonable to pay less than you would for a Kennel Club registered dog of the same breed.

ME, ME, ME!

You may find when viewing a litter of puppies that one or two will appear to be saying 'take me, take me' as they crawl all over you. On the other hand, there may be one or two that have squeezed into a corner not wanting to interact with you or, indeed, the other puppies.

At about four weeks of age when the puppies' senses are all functioning and they are able to move around they will start to play with each other and with their mother. They will start to learn through play, among other things, bite inhibition, dominance and submissive behaviours to their litter mates and their mother. The bolder puppies are likely to be the ones that 'choose' you.

The puppies that have a stronger character may prove to be difficult for a first-time owner. They may be more difficult to train and take more liberties at home. That does not mean the puppy is 'dominant' over humans – dogs are not dominant over humans (see the recommended reading list in 'Taking it further'). If he has been the bully of the litter, he may be a bully with other dogs later on. Alternatively, the shy puppy, which is usually the one that the dominant puppies have 'picked on', may appear scared of the outside world and everything he meets in it. As a general rule, if you are looking for a pet or companion dog, find a puppy with a temperament somewhere between the two extremes.

However, the temperament you see in a puppy is not necessarily the temperament you will get when he is an adult. There are many things that can change a dog's character. To name but a few: a dog with a bold character may become less bold, even introvert, if he is not socialized at the right time and in the right way; or if an inappropriate, harsh method of training is used; if he's abused physically or psychologically by his owner or a member of the family; if he has cold, damp living conditions; if he is fed an inappropriate diet; if he is attacked by another dog or is exposed to lengthy periods of unpleasant stimuli such as loud noises, fireworks, bird scarers, or gun shots. In fact, there are a multitude of possibilities that can change a bold dog into a scared dog. Conversely, a puppy that is an introvert can become more extrovert if he is socialized in the right way and at the right time; if he is trained using positive, motivational methods, and his general living conditions and treatment by the family are all positive. If his early learning experiences with you are rewarding ones and he has many good interactions with people and dogs in particular, his personality and confidence will grow.

Questions to ask, and to answer

As well as being prepared with all the questions you will need to ask the breeder, you also need to be prepared for the breeder to ask

you a lot of questions. A good breeder will care where the puppies
are going and may ask some rather searching questions.

Insight
A good breeder will want to know about you and where their
puppy is going.

They might want to know how long the puppy will be left on his
own; where he will sleep; whether you have had a dog before;
whether you are prepared to train the puppy; whether you have
children, and if so, how many and what ages; the size of your
garden and whether it's enclosed; why you chose that specific
breed, whether you have studied the breed characteristics, and
whether you intend to breed from him. If your breeder is not
interested in where the puppy is going to live, then there is a good
chance that he is not interested in what he has bred. Move on to
another breeder.

MALE OR FEMALE

More often than not, when it comes down to deciding on a male
or female, it usually boils down to personal preference. On the
other hand, some people just don't care as long as they get a
puppy! Dogs have a very acute sense of smell, so an adolescent
or adult male will detect the scent of a bitch in season from some
distance away. This may have the effect of the dog not eating and
loss of toilet training. Some males will go to any length to get to
the source of the scent, so the owners must take precautions and
ensure their dog cannot escape from the garden. Neutering, of
course, will permanently solve the 'problem', but should not be
embarked on too early.

Some people prefer bitches, because they are smaller than
the male of the breed and some people believe that bitches are
more compliant and easier to train. In fact, compliance and
trainability depend very much on breed characteristics, how you
have socialized the puppy and the method you use to train the
puppy.

Bitches usually come into season twice a year, and the first season can start as young as six months of age. A season will last about 18 days during which time the vulva swells and exudes a bloody discharge. Midway through the oestrus (season) the bitch will be receptive to a male dog, and may be as intent to get to a male as a male is in getting to her! They can have a phantom pregnancy after their season has finished; they may collect toys and even guard them. Some bitches go as far as producing milk during a phantom pregnancy. A bitch's personality may also change when she is coming up to a season and she may go off her food and become snappy and irritable with other dogs, or she may become quieter and retreat to her bed wanting to be left alone. If any of these things happen to your bitch, speak to your vet for advice and possibly medical help.

Both males and females can suffer from medical problems later in life if they are not neutered, including different types of cancer for both dog and bitch, and a potentially life-threatening infection called pyometra in bitches, and which is not always detectable until it is too late.

If you already have a dog at home and you are looking for a second, then the best match is with dogs of the opposite gender. So if you have a male, the best choice to make when looking for a puppy is a female, although you must ensure that one, or both, are neutered at the right age.

TO WORK OR NOT TO WORK

There are many breeds of dog that are classified as working dogs; Border Collies, Retrievers and Spaniels to name but three. Most working breeds have two bloodlines, one for the working dog and the other for the show dog. A dog bred to perform a job of work will have been bred for the specific behaviours that give him the ability to do that job and will come from generations of working dogs. The dog bred for the show ring will have been bred for his looks and conformation and will probably come from generations of show dogs. While show dogs still retain their working instincts, generally they have been somewhat diluted by the generations of breeding for looks rather than their working ability. If you are looking for a pet or companion dog, find a breeder that breeds for the show ring, or from lines of dogs who have been bred for the ring, so the dog has less of the working instinct.

> **Insight**
> You will need to provide extra exercise and stimulation for a 'working' dog.

If you buy a puppy which has come from generations of dogs bred to work, then you are likely to end up with a dog that has the desire and need to work, which you may not be able to satisfy.

DOUBLE TROUBLE

Even if you are an experienced owner or trainer, do not be persuaded or tempted to buy two puppies from the same litter. Looking after and training one puppy can be difficult enough, but with two it will be more than twice as difficult.

> **Insight**
> Resist the temptation to buy two puppies from the same litter.

If the puppies are from the same litter, the bond between them can be very strong to the point where they cannot bear to be parted from each other, and in many cases getting them to pay attention to you may be very difficult indeed.

BUYING A CROSS-BREED

You may of course prefer to buy a dog that is not a pedigree. Many breeders advertise litters for sale in local newspapers or advertise in veterinary surgeries. Just because the dog has no pedigree does not mean the breeder should take any less care over rearing the puppies; you should still insist on seeing the dam.

Apart from hereditary ailments, you should still ask pertinent questions.

Places to avoid

PUPPY FARMS

Unfortunately, there are unscrupulous breeders who prey on people's sympathies and sell puppies that have been raised in less than ideal conditions. Puppy farms have had bad publicity and rightly so. These are establishments that breed from a bitch every time she comes into season until she is physically and mentally worn out. When you go to see a puppy, that's usually all you will see; just one puppy. You won't be able to make a choice from a litter and you won't be able to see the dam. The mental and physical health of the puppies is usually suspect, they may be covered in fleas, are unlikely to have been wormed and have had no socialization. A puppy like this will tug on your heartstrings but given that the pup has had a really bad start in life, you may find yourself with a sickly, nervous puppy that will grow up to be a sickly, nervous dog. Puppies that have been bred on a 'puppy farm' are often sold from a person's home, to persuade you that you are buying from a reputable source. There will be a story as to why you can't see the dam. People who can be this unscrupulous can be very persuasive. Ask questions and if you have any doubts, walk away.

Insight
Do not buy from a 'puppy farm' or pet shop.

PET SHOPS

Pet shops may obtain puppies from puppy farms or breeders who have a surplus of puppies. Either way you won't know at what age the pups were taken away from their mother. There is a great risk of the puppies not being in the best of health, they may not have been wormed regularly, if at all, and are unlikely to have been socialized appropriately.

LOCAL NEWSPAPERS

Puppies are often advertised for sale in local newspapers. Some of them may be genuine but others may not. The advertisements to be suspicious of are those that offer many different breeds of puppy for sale. These may be puppy farms, or they may be a dealer who has bought unwanted puppies from different sources.

Insight
Avoid advertisements offering different breeds for sale.

The dealer may offer to bring the puppy to your home or meet you somewhere convenient. If that is the case then just say, 'Thanks, but no thanks.' This is someone with something to hide; a dealer, puppy farm, or someone who has bought an entire litter with the sole aim of making a profit.

10 THINGS TO REMEMBER

1 *Getting a puppy is a big decision – make sure you have the time, energy, finance and inclination to take one on.*

2 *Go to a reputable breeder – ask friends, your vet and other contacts in the dog world for recommendations.*

3 *Research the breed thoroughly before making a decision.*

4 *Do not buy a working breed if you are not going to be able to give it the time for exercise and training it will need.*

5 *If you are buying a pedigree puppy make sure you know what hereditary problems the breed has, and make sure all possible health checks have been carried out.*

6 *Expect to be asked a lot of questions by the breeder. If they are not interested in where their puppy is going, walk away.*

7 *Always see the dam with her puppies.*

8 *Do not buy from a pet shop or 'puppy farm'.*

9 *Do not buy two puppies from the same litter.*

10 *Think long and hard before getting a puppy – yes, I know that is the second time I have said it. That is how important it is!*

10

Where to find an older dog

In this chapter you will learn:
- *where to find an older dog*
- *where to find rescue centres*
- *about specific breed rescue.*

You may, of course, decide on getting an older dog that has
been through the puppy stage, is house-trained and has grown
out of all the puppy behaviours that some people find difficult to
deal with. Probably the most popular places to find an older dog
are national re-homing centres such as the RSPCA, The Dogs
Trust and The Blue Cross. There are many other well-known
re-homing centres around the country and lots of independently
run re-homing centres, many of which have charitable status.
For further advice, speak to the Kennel Club, or your vet or vet's
receptionist who will have details of local re-homing centres. Most
breed clubs operate their own rescue/re-homing service, so if you
want a particular breed it is a good idea to check with them. You'll
find more in 'Taking it further'.

A lot of older dogs waiting to be re-homed are indeed house-trained
and problem free. They have been put up for re-homing for a myriad
of reasons, none of which are behavioural issues. However, some
dogs are put up for re-homing because they do have behaviour
problems. Some of these you may be able to deal with – the dog is not
trained or he has not been house-trained, for example. But if not, get
in touch with an APDT trainer and ask for help, or an appropriate
class.

A lot of dogs up for re-homing are toilet-trained and problem free.

Some dogs may have had problems that are not problems in your household – perhaps the dog didn't get on with another dog in his previous home, or couldn't tolerate cats, but you don't have any other pets. But some problems could be bigger. Be sure that you have the experience and support to deal with taking on a dog with a major problem. Dogs like these are not suitable for first-time owners.

RE-HOMING CENTRES

Most re-homing centres will ask for payment. This may be a standard charge or a sliding scale depending on the age of the dog. The dog will usually be neutered before he leaves the centre, or they will ask you to arrange the operation within a certain period. When acquiring a dog from one of the nationally recognized re-homing centres, expect a lengthy question and answer session so the centre can be fairly sure the dog is going to a good home and the family and dog are well suited.

Before being allowed to take your chosen dog home, expect a home visit from one of their representatives. This visit will give the centre more of an insight as to where the dog will be going, to ask questions about the family and their routines, and make sure there is nothing that might pose a problem for the dog or the family, such as another dog or cat in residence (if the chosen dog is known to not get on with other dogs or cats); and that the garden is secure. It will also give you the opportunity to ask questions of the representative that you may have forgotten to ask when you visited the centre. A few weeks after you have had the dog a representative from the centre may pay another visit to your home. The purpose of this visit is to make sure the dog is being well looked after, that the owners have not found any unexpected problems with the dog and to talk about how the dog has settled in and adapted to the family's routine.

An independent re-homing centre will still make a charge for the dog but depending on how far away the new potential owners live, may not be able to make home visits. Depending on financial constraints, they may not be able to neuter the dog.

BREED RESCUE SOCIETIES

Most breeds of dog have their own rescue societies, which take in a specific breed for re-homing. When an owner of a specific breed feels they can no longer keep the dog, instead of handing it over to a national or independent re-homing centre, they may choose to hand it over to a breed rescue society. Some of these societies have contacts throughout the country, and others are relatively small and work within a comparatively small area.

Insight
If you are looking for a particular breed, check with the relevant breed club.

When a dog is handed in, the owner hands over ownership of the dog to the breed rescue society and they will then find the dog a suitable home. The original owner will have no further contact with the dog. Depending on the size of the society and the number of volunteers it has, you may or may not get a home visit.

Because the breed rescue societies often take in dogs that have been Kennel Club registered, the registration papers are kept by the society or returned to the breeder. This is to prevent new owners breeding from their new dog and selling Kennel Club registered puppies.

All the breed re-homing centres are published in the *Dog Rescue Directory* produced by the Kennel Club. They will send a copy free of charge or check with the relevant breed club and ask for contact details of your nearest rescue coordinator.

10 THINGS TO REMEMBER

1 *There are always older dogs looking for a home.*

2 *Many dogs needing re-homing are toilet-trained and problem free.*

3 *Some dogs may have problems that would not apply in a new environment.*

4 *Other dogs may have problems that make them unsuitable for first-time buyers.*

5 *Be prepared for questions on your facilities for keeping a dog (and perhaps a home visit), and your commitment to his welfare.*

6 *If you feel you can offer a dog – as opposed to a puppy – a new home there are plenty of places to look.*

7 *There are national and local re-homing centres in all parts of the country.*

8 *If you are looking for a particular breed, contact the breed society and get details of their 'rescue' service.*

9 *Breeders sometimes have older dogs – dogs that have been used for breeding and are no longer used for this.*

10 *They also have show dogs that have been 'run on' to see if they will be suitable for the showing in breed competitions. Again, the breed club may be able to give you suggestions of whom to contact.*

11

Common problems

In this chapter you will learn:
- *how to stop your dog jumping up*
- *how to teach your puppy not to bark*
- *how to curb attention-seeking behaviour.*

Of course, bringing up a puppy is not all plain sailing and you should always be prepared for when things start to go wrong.

JUMPING UP

Why do they do it?

If you have ever watched a young puppy greeting an older dog for the first time he will, if he is sensible, approach steadily and give a hello sniff, then he wiggles up to the dog's mouth and tries to lick his muzzle. This will tell the older dog that he, the puppy, knows his place and wants to be friends.

With small puppies, of course, many people encourage jumping up behaviour as firstly it is a cute puppy, and secondly it is a long way to bend down. As the puppy grows and the jumping up becomes more enthusiastic it becomes a bit of a nuisance. Also, this will have now extended to all your friends and maybe even total strangers in the street that he would like to be his friends.

It is therefore very unfair to use punitive methods to correct this behaviour. If you were trying your best to show how much you wanted someone to be your friend and they smacked you on the nose with a newspaper, or stood on your toes, I think it can be guaranteed that it would hurt your feelings even more than your person.

Insight

Try to understand why your puppy is jumping up.

From very early on it is a good idea to show the puppy what is acceptable as a greeting from a human perspective. Of course, teaching him to shake hands is an option, but it is much better to use something more appropriate such as sit and look pretty.

Start by using members of your own family, because these are the people whom he meets regularly, and on whom he can practise his skills; also you will have control over the reaction of the people he greets. Holding the puppy on a lead, and with a treat in your hand, stand still as a person approaches. When your puppy jumps, ask the approaching person to also stand still. When the puppy stops jumping, give him a treat and get the other person to walk away and re-approach. The puppy will learn to sit automatically when approached. Practise this with every family member, starting with adults, and work down to the children. You should then use friends as guinea pigs and get the puppy to practise on a range of people until this becomes second nature. (See also Chapter 5.)

The real problem is around young children who are quick, loud and fun. Do not let your puppy play chasing games with children, but give them quiet training games to play. If your puppy learns that chase games with children are a no-no, then he won't be jumping at children he meets in the park.

Unless you have a shy puppy who needs encouraging to meet people, it is not a good idea to get other people to give your dog treats when they approach or he will expect every person he meets to feed him, and this could actually increase his desire to run up to other people and jump on them for treats.

RESOURCE GUARDING

It can be funny to see a tiny puppy standing over his food bowl and guarding it from all comers. Who does he think he is? Of course, if this behaviour carries on you may have major problems when he is an adult. It is not so funny when your dog is guarding the kitchen because he has a biscuit on the floor and will not allow anyone in until he has eaten it.

From day one, many owners start by taking the puppy's dinner away and then giving it back to him. The idea behind this was to show the puppy who is boss, to let him know that you, the owner, controls his food so he had better do what he is told.

In the puppy's eyes, however, this means that you approaching his food bowl could mean the loss of his dinner, and if he has been successful in keeping people away in the past by growling and this is now not working, then snapping may be the next course of action. Think how you would feel if after a hard day's work you were presented with a nice hot dinner only to have someone snatch it away just to prove to you that they could. No one, however, feels threatened when in a restaurant the waiter approaches you with a serving dish to offer more vegetables or another helping of chips.

Insight
It is important that your dog understands that people near his food bowl are good news.

But you need to be able to approach your dog's food bowl, so what should you do instead? Prevention is better, and easier, than cure; so right from day one you need to explain to your puppy that people approaching his bowl is good news. Put half of his meal into his bowl. Let him eat it, stand near his bowl and when he has finished put the remaining part of his food in. Another idea is a more random reward. Give your dog his meal (all of it) in his bowl. Let him start eating and then walk up to the bowl and drop a tasty morsel in – a small piece of chicken, cheese or sausage – and either stand and watch him for a few seconds or carry on walking by. Do this often enough and an approaching person means that a bonus is about to be added. Instead of expecting a person to be a threat to your dog's dinner the approaching person becomes a bearer of something special.

If this is already an established problem it is important you ask your vet for a referral to a behaviourist.

BARKING

A dog that barks when left alone in the house is a major problem for the owner, as it inevitably affects the neighbours and causes friction. There is nothing more annoying than a dog next door who barks continuously when left.

When you first get your new puppy it may be the case that you have been very careful not to leave it on its own. You may even have taken a week off work to settle him in. The day then dawns when you must leave him with a nice new toy. But how stressful will it be when you go off and close the door on him?

Insight
It is important that your puppy gets used to being on his own for short periods.

If your puppy sleeps downstairs he is, of course, left for seven or eight hours on his own anyway, so why should it be a big deal to leave him during the day for a short time?

By far the best way is to start from day one and ensure that he is left every day in another room with the door closed, starting with a few minutes and building up to about half an hour. By waiting until he is asleep and then going into another room, he will wake up and realize he is on his own. If he makes a huge fuss you will have to wait until he is quiet, and has remained quiet for a few seconds before going back to him. If you can hear him moving around quietly then go in and make a fuss of him for the quiet behaviour. Increase the amount of time he is left slowly and don't always go to the same place, or he will get used to the idea that you are only upstairs because he can hear you moving around. Sometimes, go out into the garden or drive the car around for a few minutes. In this way the puppy is given confidence that you will soon be back and there is nothing to worry about.

Also, try not to make it obvious to him that you are off out without him. Of course, there are lots of things that we do before going out that the puppy will pick up on. We turn off the television, shut the windows, put on our coat and outdoor shoes, pick up the car keys and lock the door. He will soon learn that if this little ritual does not also include picking up his lead, then he is in for a boring afternoon.

We can make this far worse by adding a few clues which definitely tell him that he will be 'home alone'. Making a fuss of him and telling him we won't be long. Giving him toys and chews in his bed. Leaving the radio on, when we never usually have it on during the day. If we are worried about leaving him, he will automatically think that this is a bad thing. Don't treat him any differently prior to going out, don't make a fuss and say 'goodbye' and how much you will miss him. If you want to leave him a nice chew don't present it to him with an apology for going out, but hide it somewhere where he is most likely to find it. By building up the period he is left alone slowly, he won't become anxious when you go out and bark or chew inappropriate items (as long as he has appropriate, safe chew toys). It might also be a good idea to warn the neighbours of the arrival of a new puppy, and if you have to go out for any length of time ask them to pop in and let him out for you.

Barking at the door could be considered acceptable if the caller is a stranger; however, most dogs will bark at any knock at the door and are not easily dissuaded from it once the door is opened.

This behaviour is learned at a very early age, as a knock on the door always predicts that someone will get up and go to the door and visitors come in. Of course, in the early days the puppy is the centre of attention, and he truly believes that all visitors have come especially to see him. This causes great excitement and leads to barking. We try to stop him by holding onto his collar and saying 'no' very loudly. This increases his efforts as he is frustrated by being restrained and he thinks that you are now joining in.

What could your dog do instead?

Dogs often exhibit behaviours that owners don't want. Perhaps their dog has built up a behaviour of rushing to the door. He barks to let you know someone is there. Often the owners shout at the dog thinking he will stop the behaviour, but perhaps your dog is thinking 'Oh good, they are joining in the alert.' Instead of stopping the behaviour you are, in fact, inadvertently rewarding it! The owner asks for help and the first question an instructor will ask is 'What do you want your dog to do?' Owners will generally answer that they want the dog not to rush at the door. Seems sensible, but it's not really. If you did something and you were continually told 'no', but not told what behaviour was expected of you, how would you feel? Instead of just telling your dog 'no' when he shows a behaviour you don't want, think of an incompatible behaviour. Try to think of a behaviour that he can do instead of that behaviour. In this example (if you don't want your dog to rush to the door when someone knocks on it) you could teach him to go to his bed in the kitchen when someone knocks on the door. If he is going to his bed in the kitchen it is physically impossible for him to be going to the front door at the same time.

DIGGING

Many dogs like to dig; this is a natural canine behaviour. Some breeds are better at this than others; terriers especially excel at digging. They will also dig for somewhere cool to lie in hot weather. This behaviour has carried over into our domestic dogs that seem to dig just for recreation.

We tend to inadvertently reward digging behaviour with the very exciting game of chasing our dog around the garden, or by taking out a toy to take his mind off the lawn. This, of course, will result in your dog digging to get your attention. Call him immediately he begins to dig, and redirect him to somewhere that he can dig, and praise when he digs in the place that you want him to.

Of course, dogs also watch us digging and will sit and observe you digging and burying bulbs or plants, and are just waiting for an opportunity to get in there and find out what is so special that you need to bury it. When they dig it up we then reinforce that idea by chasing them around the garden to get the prized shrub back. It is probably better not to let them watch, or to keep them out of the garden until the next day when they may have had the digging idea replaced with dreams of next-door's cat. Remember also that bulbs (as well as plants) can be poisonous to your dog.

If your dog is a committed digger and gets huge pleasure from the act of digging, it may be as well to designate a small piece of garden to him. Rather than trying to stop him digging at all, stick a few dog biscuits in a freshly dug plot and when you catch him digging in your rose beds show him that there is nothing of value there, but you will show him where the real treasure is buried. When he starts to get the idea of digging in this area you can start to bury the biscuits a little way down, and bury some toys. Hopefully he will soon start burying things himself, but even if he doesn't, isn't it worth a little effort to save your prized begonias?

Insight

Consider giving your dog his own 'digging pit'.

If you really do not want him to dig in any part of your garden, you can always buy him a child's sandpit and a couple of bags of builders' sand for him to dig in. If you do this then make sure you cover it up at night so the local cats don't use it as a toilet.

INAPPROPRIATE PLAY

We all want our puppy to be friendly with other dogs and to have doggy friends whom he can socialize with. It is not much fun, however, when out with your new puppy if a huge adult dog comes bounding across the park, completely out of control, followed by an owner yelling, 'He only wants to play.' Your young puppy will, of course, be frightened to death. By allowing your young dog to play out-of-control games with other dogs he will grow up to believe that every dog he sees will want to play with him, and that playing involves biting at necks and ears, chasing around madly, holding the other dog on the ground and generally bullying him. If you are not careful the dog running up to, and scaring, other dogs will be yours!

When playing with another dog they should be provided with toys and encouraged to play games that involve chasing each other for the toy or playing tugging games. That way, if the other dog in the park does not have a toy it will not be of much interest.

If you own two dogs and they spend all their time playing rough games with each other, you are unlikely to be able to control their behaviour when out. Ensure that you are in control of the games and that they play much more with you than with other dogs.

Insight

If you have more than one dog, make sure that they spend time playing with you individually.

Should the older dog correct your puppy for biting too hard or just being a pest, back him up – the puppy needs to learn that this is not the way to treat older dogs and that you will not condone such behaviour. It is far better that your puppy plays with an older dog who is prepared to play games in moderation, but will tell the youngster when he has gone too far.

ATTENTION-SEEKING BEHAVIOUR

Puppies need attention. You should be paying attention to your puppy to make sure he doesn't need a wee, that he is not chewing inappropriately, that he is safe and generally content. There is nothing wrong with your puppy/dog asking for your attention if he wants a game, a cuddle, a training session. But, and this is important, he must also learn that he cannot always *have* attention. Sometimes he has to amuse himself, lie down in his bed, chew a toy, check out the garden or any of the other appropriate behaviours you have helped him learn. So when trainers refer to 'ignore attention-seeking behaviour' what they really mean is ignore *inappropriate* attention seeking or *unwanted* attention-seeking behaviour. As with children, inappropriate attention-seeking behaviour is best ignored. The trouble with this theory is that attention-seeking puppies are so cute.

How insistent your dog will be for your attention will depend on the reward the puppy gets for it. Rewards should not only be thought of as things he can eat or things he can play with. Talking to your puppy is a reward as is stroking him, scratching his ears or tummy. Even looking at him when he has diverted your attention from your favourite television programme can be considered a reward.

So what should you do? If your dog comes up to you while you are watching the television and wants a fuss, you could say hello, give him a stroke and ask him to settle (see Chapter 6 for information on 'settle'). It is not fair to always ignore your dog when he wants attention, especially if you have been away for a long period of time. You may have had a busy exciting day with your colleagues, but your dog hasn't. He has been home alone, bored and waiting for you to come in. Of course he is going to want some interaction.

Unwanted attention-seeking behaviours can include barking, chewing, tail chasing, Any new or unusual behaviours (such as the above) should be checked by your vet – they may be attention-seeking, but they may indicate an underlying health problem.

A very common behaviour problem is barking when the owner is on the telephone. This almost always gets results as it is very difficult to hold a conversation when the dog is barking and will inevitably mean that the owner has to break off the conversation if only to tell the dog to be quiet, thereby rewarding the behaviour by paying attention to it.

How then can you deal with the behaviour by ignoring it? Do not start by waiting for a real telephone call, but set up the situation. Dial your own number from your mobile phone and answer it. You can then hang up the mobile so as not to run up your phone bill. Pretend to be holding a conversation and as soon as your dog makes a noise put down the receiver and leave the room. This is just what he didn't want; remember he is after attention, not isolation. If you have a real call during this period of re-education, put the dog in another room before answering the telephone.

Or you could just take no notice of your dog while you are talking on the phone, but if he is used to getting your attention he will try harder initially.

Insight
Learned behaviours always get worse before they get better.

Chewing as an attention getter works well when your puppy is bored and wants a game. Having tried to get you to play by bringing you his toys and not getting the attention he wants, he may well play for a while on his own. When he becomes bored with the game, his teeth may inadvertently stray onto the leg of the coffee table. You will immediately jump up saying 'no! no!' and give him an alternative for his chewing activity. Now you are paying attention to the toy, which is what he wanted in the first place. He will soon learn to go straight for those items he is not meant to have, such as the TV remote, glasses case, furniture. In the case of the TV remote and such items, he will be able to instigate huge games by chasing round the house with them in his mouth and getting you to chase him.

It is important that you pay attention to the behaviours you do want. You could quietly praise him when he is lying down, or tell him how well he is doing when he is chewing one of his chew toys.

When your puppy takes items that he is not supposed to have don't be tempted to chase after him, thereby showing him that this item is of great value to you and you are prepared to indulge him in endless games of chase to regain possession. The best strategy is to walk quietly past him and carelessly drop a food treat; when he leaves the article do not grab it up and hide it or you will reinforce his belief that this is a highly prized possession that you are keen to keep for yourself. Ignore the discarded item and drop another treat a bit further away. Once the puppy has his mind on other things, quietly pick up the object of his attention (when he is not looking) and place it out of his reach. By showing no interest in it yourself he will no longer be fixated on it as a means of gaining your attention. If he then picks up a dog toy, pay great attention to that and offer to play with him. He will then be more inclined to pick up those items that he is allowed to have, as a way of making you take notice of him. Once he has learned to 'leave it' (see Chapter 6) you can ask him to leave the inappropriate item and reward him for that.

Tail chasing can elicit a lot of attention for different reasons. Tail chasing is, of course, funny and puppies can gain everyone's attention with a bit of silly behaviour. However, tail chasing can get out of control, and if you are unable to interrupt this behaviour then you may have a problem. Ask your vet to check him – it may be an anal gland problem, or other health issue. If he has no health problems, then ask your vet for a referral to a behaviourist.

WORKTOP SURFERS

Very often you need to manage a situation until you can train your dog in the behaviour you require. A dog jumping up at the worktops for food is one of these occasions.

All dogs will try to find free food when they can; very young dogs are often hungry, and the smell of food being prepared on the work surface is too hard to resist! The problem is usually at its peak at around five to six months of age, as the young dog grows tall enough to reach the counter. Crumbs and scraps falling on the floor further reinforce the behaviour. You may find yourself constantly telling your dog to 'get down'.

You can use a baby-gate to keep the dog out of the kitchen (see 'Managing the environment', Chapter 7), at least when you are preparing food, or have left cooking pots in the kitchen unattended. If you are not at home then make sure that food is put away. It is too tempting to leave tasty 'people' food in areas that your young dog can reach.

There are no 'quick fixes' for established behaviour problems. Managing the environment can help, as can teaching your dog alternative behaviours. The longer the behaviour has been established, the more time and patience will be required to change it. If you are going to change your dog's behaviour, consistency is essential. If you are teaching him 'don't jump up' and occasionally he is allowed to jump up, or he is unable to find food except occasionally when you forget to put it away, then you are undoing all your hard work. Occasionally 'rewarding' unwanted behaviour will take you back to square one in your training; in fact, it will make the behaviour even more likely to occur.

A warning! Some owners are advised to use noisy apparatus such as pebbles in cans, baking trays or even water-squirting bottles to stop unwanted behaviour. Although they may seem harmless at the time, many dogs can be traumatized by their use and your relationship with your dog may be damaged. It can be very difficult for a dog to recover from such trauma. Please seek professional help and even then question the methods: are they suitable for your dog?

10 THINGS TO REMEMBER

1 *Prevention is better than cure – this is particularly true of problem behaviours.*

2 *Once your dog has experienced a reward for a behaviour it can be difficult to 'cure' the problem.*

3 *Consistency in rules, routine, cue words and expectations will all help your dog understand what is expected of him.*

4 *Manage your dog's environment, such as baby-gates in the house, and avoid situations that might allow behaviour you don't want.*

5 *When your dog is showing behaviours that you do not want, think how you might be unintentionally rewarding it, and stop!*

6 *Instead of continually telling your dog 'no', think of an alternative behaviour, and ask him to do that.*

7 *Teach your puppy that people near his food bowl are good news.*

8 *Practise 'swapping' things, don't just take an item. Let him learn that giving things to you is worth his while, and not a threat.*

9 *If your dog likes to dig, provide him with an area in the garden where he can dig.*

10 *Keep temptation out of your dog's way – do not leave food on the worktop.*

12

The older dog

In this chapter you will learn:
- *how to care for an older dog*
- *how to look for the signs of ageing*
- *how to exercise as appropriate for your dog's age.*

Different breeds tend to age at different rates. As a generalization the bigger the dog, the earlier the onset of old age. With some slight adjustments to their lifestyle most dogs are able to stay active and fit during their later years. Signs of old age are greying around the muzzle, an increase or decrease in weight, sleeping longer and deeper, tooth decay, thinning coat, maybe becoming more intolerant of other pets or of being groomed. However, all of the above can be caused by things other than age, so if in doubt please talk to your vet and get your dog's health checked.

Insight
Always get your dog checked by the vet when ageing symptoms appear.

Feeding

Because the older dog may take less exercise their total energy requirement may be less.

- *Use good quality food. Food of high energy and nutrient density means your dog can eat smaller meals and still obtain the essential nutrients. .*
- *It is a good idea to divide the daily food intake into several small, highly digestible meals.*
- *Ensure that the diet you use is a balanced one with the correct vitamin and mineral content.*

Exercise

The older dog still enjoys and requires regular, appropriate, exercise.

- *Rather than one long strenuous walk, take your dog for two or three shorter walks.*
- *Some short-haired dogs might appreciate a coat to keep them warm.*
- *If your dog enjoys swimming make sure he is dried thoroughly afterwards, and do not allow him to swim if the weather is particularly cold.*
- *When throwing a toy or ball for your older dog, do not throw it too high, as your dog may twist as he jumps and could injure muscles or ligaments. He will tire more easily, so shorter throws for less time are more appropriate.*
- *When the weather is hot make sure that your dog does not get overheated or dehydrated.*

Training

Keeping the brain active may delay signs of dementia. Despite the saying, many older dogs are capable of learning new tricks, or perhaps improving on old ones.

Insight
Keep your older dog's mind active.

Your older dog will probably appreciate working with you on exercises that he is still physically capable of doing. For example:

▶ *Retrieve – but not for too long, or too far.*
▶ *Give a paw.*
▶ *Touch a target.*
▶ *Stay or wait – but in a position of his choice. Sitting, for example, may not be a comfortable position. And do not expect him to stay or wait for too long.*
▶ *Recall – again, not too many or from too far away.*

Tailor any exercises to how your dog is feeling on the day. If he is a bit stiff one day, then don't expect him to do repetitions of sits and downs. He will probably try to do them because he wants to succeed, but he may pay for it later. It is for you to be conscious of his limitations and not push him too far.

A lot of older dogs go deaf, or suffer a partial hearing loss. To help him cope, ensure that he understands hand signals as well as the usual verbal cues.

....
Insight
    Teach your older dog hand signals.
....

It won't matter how many times you ask your dog to 'sit' if he can't hear you, but if he has a hand signal then he will be able to understand what is required. Make sure he understands hand signals for all his regular behaviours – including 'be clean' and 'settle' – before he goes deaf. Yes, you can teach him once he is deaf, but a bit of forethought will make life easier for everyone. If his eyesight is poor, make sure the hand signals are large ones and easier for him to interpret.

If your older dog has problems learning new things, or worse, forgets the cues and behaviours that he has known for years, then he may be suffering from dementia. Talk to your vet about medical support that might help him cope. You can also help your dog by keeping to a routine that he is used to, and avoiding too many changes to his living arrangements. Have patience with your older dog; he may need extra time to do things now.

Health

Just like humans, as they get older dogs can be affected by ill health. Always err on the side of caution, and if your dog seems unwell, visit your veterinary surgeon. Although many of these problems are blamed on old age, modern veterinary medicine means that there are interventions that can at least slow down the progression of problems.

Here are a few ailments to watch for:

▶ *stiffness of joints*
▶ *bad eyesight (cataracts)*
▶ *bad breath*
▶ *lumps or growths*
▶ *deafness*
▶ *confusion*
▶ *incontinence.*

Any sudden changes in your dog's behaviour should be checked out by your vet as soon as possible.

Insight
Any behavioural changes should be checked by your vet.

With regular veterinary checks, good diet, some medical support and a knowledgeable and caring owner, dogs can live long and happy lives.

10 THINGS TO REMEMBER

1   *Different breeds tend to age at different rates. Generally the larger the dog, the earlier the onset of old age.*

2   *Most dogs like routine, but this is even more important for the older dog.*

3   *Older dogs still enjoy a walk, but a few short walks each day are better for them than one strenuous walk.*

4   *Older dogs will benefit from having their food divided into smaller, more frequent meals.*

5   *Use a good quality food so smaller portions will give him all the nutrition he needs.*

6   *It is important to keep the older dog's brain active. It is not true that 'you can't teach an old dog new tricks'!*

7   *There are health indications of old age, but they can be caused by other things. Get your dog vet-checked rather than assume the symptoms are caused by age.*

8   *Medical support is available for lots of the health issues associated with old age. Talk to your vet and get regular check-ups for your older dog.*

9   *Be patient – your older dog is probably not going to be as quick as he was at getting around or understanding things.*

10 *An older dog can still enjoy a happy and (relatively) active life.*

13

Recipes for your dog

In this chapter you will learn:
- *how to cook the best training treats*
- *how to cook your own dog biscuits.*

Shop-bought treats can be high in sugar, chemicals and preservatives. Too many can have a detrimental effect and also put weight on your dog. Also, shop-bought treats can be rather bland and, particularly when competing with environmental distractions, training something like a recall demands special rewards. Below are some home-made treats that your dogs will love.

Cheesy chomps
2 cups wholemeal flour
1 heaped teaspoon garlic powder
1 teaspoon brewers' yeast
1 cup grated cheese
1 egg
1 cup water

- ▶ *Mix the flour, garlic and brewers' yeast together, then stir in other ingredients.*
- ▶ *Knead the dough well, then roll out to $\frac{1}{4}$ inch thickness.*
- ▶ *Using a pastry cutter or knife, cut into shapes and place on a greased baking tray.*
- ▶ *Bake for 30 minutes at 150°C/gas mark 2 or until lightly browned.*
- ▶ *Store in an airtight box or tin.*

Liver cake
1 lb liver
1 beaten egg
1 lb self-raising flour
2 × garlic cloves crushed (optional)

▶ *Liquidize the liver.*
▶ *Add the flour and beaten egg.*
▶ *Cook in the oven on a medium heat until the middle is firm.*
▶ *Cool on a rack.*
▶ *Keep some in a sealed container in the fridge for immediate use and freeze the rest, as it does not keep well.*

Home-made dog biscuits
8 oz sausage meat
2–3 fl oz weak stock or water
8 oz plain wholemeal flour

▶ *Preheat oven to 180°C/350°F/gas mark 4.*
▶ *Mix the sausage meat and flour with the stock to form a stiff dough.*
▶ *Roll out on a floured surface to $\frac{1}{2}$ inch thickness, cut into squares, or roll into mini sausages.*
▶ *Place on an ungreased baking sheets and bake for 30–50 minutes depending on their size. Take care not to burn, but they need to be hard. Cool before serving.*

Dog biscuits
1 lb wholemeal flour
1 egg
1 oz melted lard
$\frac{1}{2}$ beef stock cube, crumbled
$\frac{1}{2}$ pint milk, or milk/water mixture
$\frac{1}{2}$ lb cooked ox liver

▶ *Mince the liver.*
▶ *Mix all the ingredients together and add the liquid.*
▶ *Roll out to just over $\frac{1}{4}$ inch thick.*

- ▶ *Cut out with a two-inch cutter or into squares.*
- ▶ *Bake at 100°C in a slow oven for about two hours until crisp.*

Dog biscuits

3 oz wholemeal flour
$\frac{1}{2}$ oz fat or dripping
$1\frac{1}{2}$ pints milk
2–3 fl oz weak stock or water
2 tablespoons grated cheese
$\frac{1}{2}$ beef stock cube

- ▶ *Rub the fat into the flour.*
- ▶ *Add the well-crumbled stock cube and grated cheese.*
- ▶ *Mix with milk (or milk mixture) into a stiff dough.*
- ▶ *Roll out $\frac{1}{4}$ inch thick and cut into squares.*
- ▶ *Put on a floured baking sheet and bake in moderately hot oven (180°C) for 45 minutes.*
- ▶ *When cold, store in an airtight tin.*

Liver treats

1 lb liver
1 clove garlic

- ▶ *Bring the garlic and liver to boil in a little water, simmer for five minutes until cooked through.*
- ▶ *Drain on kitchen paper and cut into small pieces.*
- ▶ *Spread on a baking sheet and bake at about 150°C for about half an hour.*
- ▶ *Turn off oven and leave until cold.*
- ▶ *This doesn't keep very well so freeze what you are not going to use immediately.*

Tuna training treats

2 × 6 oz cans of tuna in water – do not drain
2 eggs
1–$1\frac{1}{2}$ cups wholemeal flour
1 teaspoon garlic powder

- ► *Mash the tuna and water in a bowl with a fork and then liquefy in a blender or food processor.*
- ► *Add extra drops of water if needed to liquefy completely.*
- ► *Pour into a bowl and add the flour and garlic powder. The consistency should be like a cake mix.*
- ► *Spread on a greased baking tray.*
- ► *Bake at 180°C for 15 minutes.*
- ► *Use a pizza cutter or knife and cut into tiny squares. This recipe freezes well.*

Taking it further

Useful organizations

Association of Pet Behaviour Counsellors
PO Box 46, Worcester WR8 9YS. Tel: 01386 751151
www.apbc.org.uk

Association of Pet Dog Trainers, UK
PO Box 17, Kempsford GL7 4WZ. Tel: 01285 810811
www.apdt.co.uk

The Blue Cross
Shilton Road, Burford, Oxfordshire OX18 4PF. Tel: 01993 822651
www.bluecross.org.uk

The Dogs Home Battersea
4 Battersea Park Road, London SW8 2AA. Tel: 0171 622 3626
www.dogshome.org

The Dogs Trust
17 Wakley Street, London EC1V 7LT. Tel: 0171 837 0006
www.dogstrust.org.uk

The Kennel Club
1–5 Clarges Street, Piccadilly, London W1A 8AB.
Tel: 0171 493 6651/629 5828
www.the-kennel-club.org.uk

Royal Veterinary College
Camden Campus, Royal College Street, London NW1 0TU.
Tel: 0171 468 5000

RSPCA
Causeway, Horsham, West Sussex RH12 1HG. Tel: 01403 264181
www.rspca.org.uk

The UK Registry of Canine Behaviourists
North Lodge, North Street, Winkfield SL4 4SY. Tel: 01344 883955
www.ukrcb.org

Accredited courses

Association of Pet Dog Trainers, UK
PO Box 17, Kempsford GL7 4WZ
www.apdt.co.uk

COAPE
PO Box 6, Fortrose, Ross-shire IV10 8WB. Tel: 0800 783 0817
www.coape.co.uk

Recommended reading

Burch & Bailey (1998) *How Dogs Learn,* Howell Book House Inc.
Donaldson, J. (1996) *The Culture Clash,* James and Kenneth
  Publishers.
Eaton, B. (2002) *Dominance: Fact or Fiction,* Barry Eaton.
McConnell, P. (2003) *Other End of the Leash,* Random House Inc.
Parry, P. (2005) *Patsy Parry's Puppy Problems! The good, the bad
  and the downright ugly,* Crosskeys Select.
Pryor, K. (2002) *Don't Shoot the Dog,* Ringpress Books.
Rugaas, T. (1997) *On talking terms with dogs: Calming Signals,*
  Legacy By Mail Inc.
Whitehead, S. (1999) *Hands Off!,* Alpha.
Whitehead, S. (2003) *Puppy Training for Kids,* Kenilworth Press Ltd.
Whitehead, S. (2004) *The Puppy Survival Guide,* Alpha.
Woodcock, D. (2002) *Preventing Puppy Problems,* DogSense
  Publications.

All books available through Crosskeys Books at
www.crosskeysbooks.co.uk

Index